The
Wisdom
of
St. Patrick

The Wisdom of St. Patrick

of

St. Patrick

— ♣ —

Inspirations from the
Patron Saint of Ireland

GREG TOBIN

BALLANTINE BOOKS • NEW YORK

A Ballantine Book
Published by The Ballantine Publishing Group

Copyright © 1999 by Greg Tobin and The Reference Works

Library of Congress Cataloging-in-Publication Data
Tobin, Greg.
   The wisdom of St. Patrick / Greg Tobin. — 1st ed.
      p.   cm.
   Includes bibliographical references.
   ISBN 0-345-43297-5 (hardcover : alk. paper)
   1. Patrick, Saint, 373?–463?—Meditations.   I. Title   II. Title:
Wisdom of Saint Patrick.
BR1720.P26T63   1999
270.2'092—dc21
[B]   98-46505
                                                                               CIP

Text design by H. Roberts Design

Manufactured in the United States of America

First Edition: March 1999

10 9 8 7 6 5 4 3 2 1

This book is dedicated to my sons,
Patrick Alexander Tobin
and Bryan Gregory Tobin,
with love and deepest respect.

God has appointed me as an apostle and teacher
to proclaim the Good News, and it is for this reason
that I suffer these things.

—2 TIMOTHY 1:11–12

Ego Patricius, peccator rusticissimus et
minimus omnium fidelium . . .

—THE CONFESSION OF ST. PATRICK

Hear all ye who love God, the holy merits
Of the Bishop Patrick, a man blessed in Christ;
How, on account of his good actions, he is likened
    unto the angels,
And for his perfect life, is counted equal to the Apostles.

—SECUNDINUS, *HYMN OF ST. PATRICK*

He conquered by steadfastness of faith, by glowing zeal,
and by the attractive power of love.

—NEANDER

CONTENTS

ACKNOWLEDGMENTS

I am grateful to many people who contributed materially and spiritually to the composition of this book. First and foremost, Harold Rabinowitz and his company, The Reference Works, shaped the original proposal to the publisher, provided excellent reference materials and expert clerical support, criticized and edited the writing, sagely guided the entire process from the barest germ of an idea (in fact, only a working title) to the finished product. Harold, my coauthor in spirit and in fact, also discovered one of the rarest as well as the most beautiful and seminal books on the subject, *The Life of St. Patrick, Apostle of Ireland* by M. F. Cusack, the "Nun of Kenmare," which contains the complete Latin versions of the saint's own writings, as well as some wonderful nineteenth-century illustrations. I cannot thank Harold and his staff at The Reference Works enough.

A special note of appreciation is due Alexander Hoyt

who, as literary agent, friend, and colleague in the book-publishing business, first approached me about a very different project; despite his best efforts to convince me to embark upon that book, he got this instead, and he found just the right home for it.

Elizabeth R. Zack, Judith Curr, and Linda Grey of Ballantine Books decided to publish *The Wisdom of St. Patrick*. Elizabeth, as my hands-on, ever-available sponsor, offered sure and sensitive editorial guidance throughout the process, graciously reading primitive and incomplete drafts, pointing me toward logical and complete thought and correct grammar. She kept me on track and ensured the viability of the project within the house. Neither her patience nor her enthusiasm ever dimmed. I could not have hoped for a better editor. Judith as publisher and Linda as president both oversaw the publishing effort in their consummately intelligent and professional manner.

The staff at Seton Hall University's Walsh Library played a crucial role in the birth of this book. They helped me navigate the stacks and locate as much research material as is available at their beautiful facility in my own hometown.

Monsignor William Noé Field, poet, author, teacher, and priest, who presides over the Special Collections Department at the university library, permitted me access to the MacManus Irish History and Literature Collection, a trove of Irish historical books and papers. He hovered willingly but discreetly when I worked there, offering counsel and the more than occasional translation of Latin words and texts. He is one of the most vigorous, devout, and joyful octogenarians one could ever expect to meet.

I must not forget to thank Howard Frisch, book antiquarian extraordinaire, for supplying a copy of Bury's *Life*.

My wife, Maureen Patricia Tobin, put up with my mental excursions to ancient Ireland and Britain with her usual bemused tolerance. My elder son, Patrick, unknowingly inspired the process a long time ago by virtue of carrying the saint's name. My younger son, Bryan, quietly supported me with his humor and honesty, for which I admire him. And fellow passengers on the crowded New Jersey Transit commuter train to and from New York City endured my stony concentration, shifting elbows, and precariously balanced coffee cup on many an early morning as I wrote to meet deadline.

Finally, I must acknowledge my debt to the many authors and scholars who have gone before. There is more detailed information about translations and sources later on, but I wish to say here that I am in their spiritual and material debt, every one of them: I know that St. Patrick blessed their lives with his living presence, as he has blessed mine.

INTRODUCTION

     rom the forbidding coast of western Britain across
the coldly turbulent Irish Sea, Patrick came to
Hibernia—*extras partes,* the "most distant places,"
in his words—first as a boy and a slave, then as a man and
a bishop. The Romans had not dared to conquer this wild
island by might of arms, but Patrick, a Roman himself,
sought his mission and succeeded where no general or
statesman ever had: to win the souls of the Irish for Christ,
his King.

    Magonus Sucatus Patricius, whom we know as St.
Patrick, the Apostle and Patron Saint of Ireland, speaks to
us down through fifteen centuries as boldly and defini-
tively today as he must have to those who listened to him
preach the gospel of Christ, haltingly yet ardently in an
adopted tongue among the pristine, pagan hills and lakes
of a country at the outermost edge of the world known to
the Romans. Like Moses, the stutterer who saw the very

face of God and carried the tablets down from the mountain, or St. Paul, the tortured soul whose universal evangelical zeal has never been surpassed, Patrick stands for something beyond the realm that we, on the cusp of the twenty-first century, consider "normal."

Yet there can be no doubt that he was a man, saint or not. He vociferously proclaimed his own imperfection and unworthiness, acknowledged and defended himself against the hatred of accusers in his own country, boasted about the thousands of Irish whom he baptized and brought into the Church of Christ, excommunicated the violators of Christian innocents with ringing, righteous anger, claimed no special miraculous powers that others imputed to him in later times yet saw many visions, and sought the protection and guidance of his Divine Father in a "mission impossible" about four hundred years after the death of Jesus of Nazareth.

Through the strongly heard echo of his own voice in the unique written record—two relatively brief documents translated into our language from his own rustic Latin—we grasp his message to us, the children of God in a later age. These two texts are, in fact, the oldest documents in Irish history and the sole contemporary witness to Patrick's life. Unlike other apocryphal saints, such as the lamented St. Christopher, we know for a fact that St. Patrick existed— and we know not very much more than what he recorded about himself.

Like his fifth century of the Common Era, within the thousand-year-old empire of Rome and at its embattled fringes, ours is an age of discontinuity, disintegration, and disconnection, a time of dying empires. Might it be the beginning of another Dark Age? There is generally conceded to be an overload of information that threatens to bury us and distract us from the purpose of our very existence: as posited by the Christian faith, to live among and love our fellow human beings for a brief interlude on this green planet before an eternal existence in an unknowable realm, be it a heaven or a hell. Inexorable forces within and without our "Western empire" have created cultural fissures that are irreparable by the hand of man: wars and genocide and racial "purification," famine and floods and droughts, economic and political crises. We are overwhelmed and numbed by the sheer mass of bad news that we hear daily, hourly, by the minute through a multiplicity of media. Further, in daily life, we are tuned in and turned on to so many commercial, cultural, and sensory impressions that, after a while, become almost meaningless. Yet we resist the conclusion that life itself therefore becomes meaningless.

Why does the death by misadventure of a divorced Princess of Wales move otherwise stoical, if not cynical foreigners—who never in their lives crossed her superfashionable path, and could never hope to do so—to feel a deep and genuine loss?

Why do tremors in corrupt East Asian financial markets cause fear and trembling on Wall Street and force a frantic flurry of political and economic reaction in otherwise healthy, comparatively stable Western nations?

Why are people of every nation and faith compelled at least to listen to the pronouncements of an aging pontiff of an ancient, riven church that some fear teeters on collapse yet claims adherents on every continent, numbering at least one billion souls?

Why do the Western powers gird their loins against random nuclear and terrorist attacks from perceived "barbarian" enemies from the East—Iran, Iraq, perhaps Pakistan or India—yet deal cash and weaponry under the table with those same so-called outlaws for precious oil and other short-term gains?

In our own personal lives we experience crises—less earth-shattering, perhaps, but often even more profound because they are so closely felt: the loss of a parent or child, the illness of a family member or close friend, financial and career setbacks, mental and emotional instability, alcoholism or other addiction, the disruption of a relationship. Who does not have these problems in one form or another every day—or, if not the immediate problem, the aftershock, which might still be echoing from childhood or a long-buried issue?

Our own late-second-millennium world, an age experienced at both an intensely personal and a distinctly universal level, can benefit from the experience of the saint who lived at what he was certain was the end time. I do not share that belief (with Patrick or with some contemporary evangelical Christians or other millennial sects); however, I do share the sense of urgency that is clearly evident in the message of the Apostle of Ireland. It is never too early, nor too late, to experience spiritual renewal and healing.

I remember that from the moment, a few years ago, when I discovered (as had many others before me) that St. Patrick had left for us a written record—that, indeed, his powerful voice speaks to us today—I was stimulated to learn more about him. I had grown up with distinct memories and impressions of the legendary saint gained from little *Lives of the Saints* books and holy cards: bearded, mitered, shamrock in hand, banisher of snakes and worker of many miracles, enemy of druidism, confessor to Irish kings. I believed that Patrick was the first Christian to set foot on the island. Yes, I remembered tales of his captivity and slavery, but little did I realize that most of the rest of his "biography" was wholly made up. Despite centuries of historical research and analysis, we have precious little reliable record of his life.

But we do have *The Confession of St. Patrick* and *The Letter to the Soldiers of Coroticus*, unmistakable Patrician documents. There is no doubt among the scholarly community that these were written by his own hand and preserved by manuscript copyists. It is a true miracle that these records have survived for a millennium and a half.

St. Patrick's voice rings clearly through the ages. His was a passionate, pious, deeply held faith in the teachings of the early Catholic Church. Through the Latin Bible (a pre-Vulgate translation in common use among the churchmen of Britain) he absorbed the teachings of Jesus Christ and the apostles. He must have been an especial reader of St. Paul's epistles, based on the frequency of quotations and similarity of language in Patrick's writing. No scholar himself—a self-proclaimed "rustic" and "ignoramus"—the missionary bishop nonetheless was an excellent student in his mature years. He learned the Scriptures as a handbook for salvation.

His language, various translators tell us, was imperfect, imprecise, at times almost incomprehensible. He was no rhetorician; he missed that class. So, he speaks from the heart, in a way few, if any, writers of the late classical age (e.g., St. Augustine) did. He could not do otherwise, for, as he tells us in no uncertain terms, he knows only how to speak the truth in blunt, even crude, everyday language.

St. Patrick's spirituality is simple, direct, practical, as earthy as it is mystical, not so much Roman Catholic as baseline Christian, not so much Irish as truly universal (catholic with a small *c*). Yet he certainly operated within the framework of the ancient Church of Britain, with strong ties to Rome; he was no freelance, as his contemporary detractors apparently accused him of being, nor a proto-Protestant, as some later writers argued.

Every serious study of the life and influence of this saint called Patrick begins with a series of disclaimers about the scarcity and unreliability of primary sources: "Although there is no doubt that Patrick was a real historical character, and although we have two pieces of writing from his hand which tell us much about himself, the reconstruction of his life has always been, and still is, a matter of extraordinary difficulty." [Hanson, *Life and Writings*, p. 12] In an authoritative edition of the extant works, we read:

> St. Patrick was not a man of letters. Whatever he wrote was wrested from him by the circumstances of his life and the demands of his episcopal office. What remains of his writings are two complete letters, some fragments from other letters, and—probably his own in good part—a set of canons or rules of ecclesiastical discipline. These, together with the hymn of St. Secundinus in honor of St. Patrick and the so-called *Lorica* of St. Patrick, are the earliest documents of the Irish Church that have survived. [Bieler, *Works*, p. 8]

Scholars have debated, retranslated, analyzed, hypothesized, claimed, disputed, wondered, and worried over these few ancient texts in Latin that, along with early Irish writings, with accumulated legend and lore, provide what little specific biographical information we have about the man and his mission among the Irish.

The first full-length study of the saint that I read was *The Life of St. Patrick and His Place in History* by J. B. Bury, M.A., a Cambridge don and classical scholar of the highest order. It is difficult to find in its original edition. I was privileged to have access to the book in the MacManus Irish History and Literature Collection at Seton Hall University, and later to obtain a copy of my own. Originally published in London by Macmillan in 1905, this book is a sincere effort by a historian to be thorough and objective about a subject that was "wrapped in obscurity, and this obscurity was [in turn] encircled by an atmosphere of controversy and conjecture." [Bury, p. v]

Bury was, in fact, first attracted to the subject "not as an important crisis in the history of Ireland, but, in the first place, as an appendix to the history of the Roman Empire, illustrating the emanations of its influence beyond its own frontiers; and, in the second place, as a notable episode in the series of conversions which spread over northern Europe the religion which prevails today." [Bury, p. v]

Bury, like virtually every important writer on Patrick, first approached the saint from an oblique angle. He was inevitably drawn in by the personality and circumstance of the man, which inform the sparse written record as well as the accreted legends and miracle stories. He also felt it necessary to counter the "unmistakable ecclesiastical bias" of Dr. J. H. Todd's biographical treatise, *St. Patrick, Apostle of Ireland* (1864), which effectively promoted the saint as the first Protestant. Bury, very much like the scholars of the mid-twentieth century, proclaims the strictest objectivity, saying, "I will not anticipate my conclusions here, but I may say that they tend to show that the Roman Catholic conception of St. Patrick's work is, generally, nearer to historical fact than the views of some anti-Papal divines." [Bury, pp. vii–viii]

This was the first I had heard of such controversies and I became hooked. I later learned in more detail of Dr. Todd's controversial point of view, of the "two Patricks" theory, the confusion with Palladius who was probably the first Christian bishop sent to the Irish—possibly by Pope Celestine I—at some point before Patrick's appointment. I would also learn about the problems of chronology that put sober-minded scholars of the past half century at odds with each other.

So, I put myself in Professor Bury's capable hands and thus journeyed to the late Roman Empire in the company of an expert tour guide. I acquired the basics of early twentieth-century scholarship, which undergirded my readings from that point on.

Apart from numerous traditions and legends about Patrick still promulgated in local oral accounts and books of stories for younger readers, historians are dependent on the two crucial documents, his *Confession* and *Letter* (sometimes called the *Epistle*). Scholars agree that these are authentic but have differed as to their purpose and their implications.

Even as the experts question and dispute the credibility of the evidence—to say nothing of conclusions drawn therefrom—their work is unfailingly and intensely interesting for the nonscholar, like me, who is seeking to learn as much as possible about the man who became the revered apostle-saint.

Without necessarily engaging in those sincere and important disputations, I have decided to leap into Patrick's story and interpret freely from English-language studies available to us, knowing full well—and alerting the reader here and now—that I may be committing some errors of strict fact or rigorous historiography or even mistakes within the far wider boundaries of interpretation. However, I will be doing so with a fixed and very personal goal in mind: to take several steps closer to the St. Patrick who has meaning for me, "a sinner and the most unschooled" (as he would put it) of Patrician students. I fondly hope that my sins are not mortal and that they do no damage to the man (I hardly think they could) or the validity and relevance of his message across the centuries.

The sources listed in the bibliography provide guidance in this fascinating spiritual and historical exploration, for others have probed the saint's mind just as I have tried to do, albeit with deeper acumen and expertise. I recommend to any reader the exciting and edifying works of scholarship from Bury to Bieler, the analyses of MacNeill and Cahill, the eminently readable narrative biography by Gallico, the newest and most exciting translations of Skinner. For a magnificent presentation of the legendary saint, the *Tripartite Life* (in mid-nineteenth-century translation), and discussion of relics and St. Patrick's Purgatory, there is M. F. Cusack's rare, beautifully illustrated volume.

I consider this book, *The Wisdom of St. Patrick*, a synthesis of various points of view concerning the saint's life and ministry, an amalgam of impressions that add up, for me, to a personal, utilitarian view; it is not the final word by a long shot. It is an enterprise that has both entertained and enlightened me in my own spiritual life.

A word or two about the structure and purpose of this book. It is neither a biography, per se, nor a new translation of the works of St. Patrick. It is not a work of original scholarship, but draws on the works of numerous Patrician historians, who are quoted and referred to throughout. The intention is to glean some relevant spiritual principles from the saint's writings and to comment thereupon, to identify how Patrick's own life and times were reflected in his writing, to find applications in our daily life, and to draw lessons that are steeped in Patrick's own reading of Scripture, which informs his every thought and deed.

Like a meditation book or spiritual workbook, this book is organized in a simple, straightforward way that I hope is useful to the reader. My intention is to provide a framework for an understanding of Patrick's words, as well as his life and times, with the hope that you will find some application to daily life in today's world at the dawn of the twenty-first century. It is a book designed to be browsed or read in small, digestible bits.

First, I have selected a quotation, either from the *Confession* or from the *Letter to the Soldiers of Coroticus*, that illustrates a theme such as faith, vocation, gratitude, anger, etc.). The excerpt gives us something to comment on, to bring out connections from Patrick's life and times that may illuminate the raw text. Where the legends that surround the life of St. Patrick as it has coursed its way through the generations seemed related to the text, I drew the connection and sought the inference. And it is possible to read these two documents penned by Patrick straight through from beginning to end without commentary; they are works that have provided millions with a source of comfort and inspiration for well over a millennium. Readers will find that Patrick's language is most often very plain, and at the same time very spiritual, rife with direct and paraphrased quotations from the New Testament. Patrick drew liberally from scriptural passages in his own writing to give voice and validity to his arguments. If this work does nothing else but bring this voice into the reader's life, it will have been a worthy undertaking.

A contemplation follows each commentary. The contemplation is intended to draw on issues from daily life, to apply the spiritual lesson represented in Patrick's writing to my own and perhaps your own life. This was one of the most intriguing exercises for me, because I found Patrick's message startlingly compelling and immediate in its impact. And with each reading of a quotation from his work, I felt more firmly that he was speaking directly to me.

Finally, in each chapter I include a prayer of my own composition, inspired by the saint's spiritual teaching. I have offered the prayer as only a suggestion for anyone who might wish to join me in an invocation to the Supreme Being, who, I believe, is the first source of anyone's existence and is clearly the inspiration and source for Patrick.

I am a Catholic layman, not a priest, not formally trained in theology or religious studies of any kind. I was born into this faith tradition, wavered and wandered as a young man, and returned to the Church as an adult, husband, and father. I have found a home in my local parish community of Our Lady of Sorrows Church in South Orange, New Jersey, that is very important to me. I love the beautiful Gothic church building and the history of the parish and its parent, the Archdiocese of Newark. It might be fair to say that I am Catholic in spite of myself, for I have been nurtured by the faith even—or especially—in times of deepest doubt and crisis. The Church has never deserted me, wherever I may have been.

My credibility, if it exists at all, lies less in any official or academic credentials than in the hoped-for quality of thinking that underlies the writing contained herein. I claim no special insight or inspiration, but I do claim the freedom to attempt to express myself as an imperfect human being. I believe that each of us who professes faith in any form possesses this same basic level of credibility. We are called to share our beliefs and strivings with each other, and it is in that spirit that I composed these brief essays and prayers.

As I have said, this book is not a biography. Rather, it is a gloss and a meditation upon the life and words of St. Patrick, as transmitted to us through scholars and translators of the past century and a half. It is not a work of original scholarship, though one hopes it might be considered an original contribution of interpretation and inspiration. This study is intended for a general readership of laymen like myself, not a professional or scholarly audience. I have sought the lessons our saint taught that apply to my own life; I have sought his company and his personal spiritual guidance; I have sought to understand the meaning of his life and his ministry for our time, so distant yet so similar to his own.

Patrick is a fascinating companion and spiritual mentor. He journeyed to wild places where none of us, in this latter day and age, can hope to go. His world was one we will never truly know, just as we can never hope to experience the world of Jesus of Nazareth, some four hundred years before Patrick's birth, or even Michelangelo's Rome a thousand years later. St. Patrick's commitment to Christ, to Church, to fellow Christians, to those who had not yet received the gospel message, was unbreakable. He was ready—and he proclaimed it in no uncertain terms—to lay down his life (though not to squander it trivially, for he knew of its potency) in the cause of truth, as he understood it.

In this way, we can draw parallels to contemporary saints and prophets such as Gandhi, Pope John XXIII, Martin Luther King, Jr., Mother Teresa, Elie Wiesel, Joseph Cardinal Bernardin; from these spiritual leaders, too, we can learn how to walk with God through this vale of tears. In Patrick's example we can learn how to obtain and cultivate the qualities of faith, hope, and love that lie at the core of his spiritual tradition.

The appeal of St. Patrick extends far beyond the shores of Ireland to every continent on earth. He is a quintessential Christian missionary whose message and personality seem to flower throughout the generations. Two hundred years after his death he was being written about as a pivotal saint responsible for the spread of the gospel to the heathens of Hibernia (as Ireland was known at the time); even then, however, there was little known of him, and the legends were repeated and recorded and preserved. The monastic communities that survived the Dark Ages were inheritors of Patrick's legacy. Throughout the Middle Ages and beyond the Renaissance, his impact on theologians and Christian pilgrims was immense. In the struggle for Irish independence, he was the patron saint to whom the people prayed for intercession in their times of trouble. In our time the St. Patrick's Day festivals and parades are occasions for pride in Irish heritage as well as for controversy.

For Irish Americans like myself, the image of St. Patrick is one of comfort as well as challenge. The avuncular bishop in his anachronistic miter and forked beard (also probably an inaccurate feature, since Magonus Sucatus Patricius was a Roman Briton), wearing a flowing green and gold chasuble, is so familiar as to blend into the woodwork or to fade into the niche at church. We were taught that he drove the snakes out of Ireland and taught the Holy Trinity with the example of the shamrock. But even through this rather bland "holy uncle" portrayal, the firm, fixed purpose of Patrick's mission still, somehow, shines through.

He was, after all, a missionary bishop who converted thousands and thousands of souls with a single-minded intensity that can be felt today. His voice—humble, angry, pleading, inspired—overrides the pallid and inaccurate portraits. And his pastoral love for the Irish imbues every word and every miracle attributed to him. There is a mutual attraction, a symbolic marriage, between St. Patrick and the Irish that has lasted for more than a millennium and a half.

My own name, Tobin, is derived from a Norman source—an emigrant, probably a soldier, of the twelfth century who came from the town of St. Aubyn. The usage was "de St. Aubyn," which became Gaelicized to Tobin, or sometimes Toíbín. According to a book of Irish names, there was no one of particular note from this family, though there were a few minor poets and the men of the family were particularly fierce in their opposition to the British.

So, indirectly—to say the least—the fruits of St. Patrick's evangelization of the Emerald Isle became grafted, presumably through marriage, to this Continental lineage that eventually planted firm roots in Ireland, then emigrated again. This time, in the 1890s, they came to North America; both of my paternal grandparents were the first in their families to be born in the United States, and they settled in Kansas City, Missouri, in the very middle of the country.

My background is very typical and could be multiplied by hundreds of thousands, if not millions. As I have related elsewhere, I was fascinated with the story of St. Patrick from my earliest grammar school days; the juvenile biography by Quentin Reynolds firmly imprinted the saint on my mind. This impression, too, is probably not unusual. And throughout my adult years I have been attuned to the saint's presence, conscious that the ubiquitous parades and corned-beef church dinners had their provenance in dark-misted times that are now all but forgotten.

I do not claim any unique relationship with Patrick or special knowledge of him, but I was curious enough to dig a little deeper into his story. Hence this book. I hope that these little comments and musings and prayers are faithful to his mission. If nothing else, his answer to the call of the Irish has touched this Irishman five hundred generations removed. Each of us can, in his own way, preserve and pass along his message to the Irish.

From a fourth-floor window of the Walsh Library at Seton Hall University, where I have conducted much of the research and writing of this book, I look down upon a statue of St. Patrick in that familiar pastoral pose: shepherd's crook resting in his left hand, his right hand upraised, white bearded, wearing a bishop's miter (anachronistically). The statue stands outside the university bookstore where students stream in and out, and there are benches where, in good weather, I have sat to read or to contemplate Patrick's presence in my life. How did he get here? That is, why a plaster statue on a faraway campus in New Jersey, U.S.A., and why did he step onto my spiritual path at this stage of my life—or I onto his—and why is his influence so deeply ingrained into the consciousness of Irish and Christian people everywhere?

It is my hope that you will find in this book answers to

such questions, and that it will be a helpful road map in your own journey with the saint.

Life, Legend, and Legacy

I

Who was he? When and where was he born? Where and by whom was he educated? How exactly did he come to Ireland, and what was the scope and authority of his mission there? What were his greatest contributions to Irish and Christian civilization? When and where did he die? "I am Patrick, a sinner, the most unlearned and least of all the faithful, and utterly despised by many."

So begins the remarkable document (in his own halting Latin words) that brings to life Magonus Sucatus Patricius, mystic and evangelist, one-time slave and wanderer, first Primate of All Ireland, fifth-century Christian missionary, patron saint and symbol of a modern European nation, eponymous guardian of magnificent cathedrals and humble Catholic parishes around the world, cause and supposed sponsor of celebratory parades in most major American urban centers—approximately a millennium and a half after his death.

> The writings of Patrick do not enable us to delineate his character, but they reveal unmistakably a strong personality and a spiritual nature. The man who wrote the *Confession* and the *Letter* had strength of will, energy in action, resolution without overconfidence, and the capacity for resisting pressure from without. It might be inferred, too, that he was affectionate and sensitive; subtle analysis might disclose other traits. But it is probable

that few readers will escape the impression that he possessed besides enthusiasm the practical qualities most essential for carrying through the task which he undertook in the belief that he had been divinely inspired to fulfill it.

A rueful consciousness of the deficiencies of his education weighted upon him throughout his career; we can feel this in his almost wearisome insistence upon his *rusticitas* [lack of learning and culture]. Nor has he exaggerated the defects of his culture; he writes in the style of an ill-educated man. His Latin is as "rustic" as the Greek of St. Mark and St. Matthew. He was a *homo unius libri* (a "one-book man"); but with that book, the Christian Scriptures, he was extraordinarily familiar. His writings are crowded with Scriptural sentences and phrases, most of them probably quoted from memory. [Bury, pp. 205–206]

Upon the foundation that Bury established, researchers of our century have erected an impressive edifice of Patrician scholarship. From T. F. O'Rahilly, whose *The Two Patricks: A Lecture on the History of Christianity in Fifth-Century Ireland* (1942) exploded the accepted version of Patrick as the immediate successor to Palladius, to the lucid works of Ludwig Bieler, R.P.C. Hanson, and Liam de Paor, to the latest (and most poetic) translation of the saint's works by John Skinner, any number of experts have told and retold and revised the story—some with more credibility and objectivity than others.

Three ancient and interrelated sources, besides his own *Confession* and *Letter*, tell the story of Patrick, each with distinct elements of embellishment and hagiography. In the latter half of the seventh century Muirchú Maccu Machteni

(d. 670?), the son of another writer, Cogitosus, composed a *Life of St. Patrick* that is the first section of the Book of Armagh, which is a collection of documents that was transcribed in Armagh in about the year 807 and now resides in the library at Trinity College, Dublin. Another biography is that of Tirechán, also contained in the Book of Armagh; it, too, was likely composed in the second half of the seventh century. Hanson writes, "It [Tirechán's *Life*] can confidently be connected with the ecclesiastical politics of his day, when the monastery and see of Armagh were claiming jurisdiction over all other churches in Ireland, in opposition to the powerful monastic connection which appealed to the Authority of [St.] Columba." [Hanson, *Life and Writings*, p. 16]

Then came the so-called *Vita Triparta*, or *Tripartite Life*, a work composed anonymously from various oral and recorded sources that carried forward the propagandistic agenda of Irish churchmen and attributed works and miracles to Patrick that are surely fiction. It is the repository of several sometimes contradictory narrative strands, which purport to give a full account of St. Patrick's life and times.

Scholar Kathleen Hughes wrote in *Early Christian Ireland*, a 1972 study of primary documents:

> Where we have several Lives of a saint like Patrick, you can also see the same saint changing his features as time goes on. Patrick's Confession shows a man toiling, insulted, persecuted, somewhat with a blot on his copybook who has repented and worked for God, and who feels hurt and indignant that his efforts should be so badly misinterpreted by his fellow-Christians. It is a completely convincing, contemporary document. Muirchú presents a heroic figure, protecting his followers,

worsting his opponents, an infallible wonder-worker: St. Patrick has become the hero of a saga. He remains so in the *Vita Triparta* [compiled during the period 895 to 902], but by now he is wringing privileges from God, concerned above all with his rights and status. Patrick's gifts to the pagan Irish described in his Confession have here become nine companions' load of gold and silver, which God promises to give to the Irish for believing. This Life demonstrates clearly that precision does not imply truth in hagiography. For instance, Muirchú says that many of the heathens perished in Patrick's encounter with Lóeghaire [Laoghaire]: the author of the *Vita Triparta* knows the number, twelve thousand. [Hughes, p. 246]

We should also credit some pre-Bury historians with appropriate skepticism. The Reverend Thomas Olden in his 1876 book, *The Epistles and Hymn of Saint Patrick,* wrote, "This treatment of the legendary element in the Tripartite and the introduction of an account of St. Patrick's Purgatory, a medieval superstition which had nothing whatever to do with him, tend to confound the truth and falsehood and mislead the enquirer." [pp. 5–6] Olden claims that his work is based on the primary records of St. Patrick's mission, and rejects the absurd miracles attributed to Patrick; they "misrepresent his mode of proceeding, from pure ignorance of what constitutes the character of a Christian missionary. Thus he curses rivers, territories, families, and individuals, for the most trivial causes, and for the same reasons prophesies evil to people, though fortunately the fulfillment does not often follow." [p. 8]

In 1889, another reverend doctor, George Gough Gubbins, asked the pertinent question "What Doctrines and

Practices Did St. Patrick Teach?" His lecture argued against an appointment by Rome of Patrick's mission and supports, more or less, Todd's previous thesis that Patrick was a proto-Protestant: "Ireland was pure in doctrine until the invasion of the heathen, and afterwards the Roman Catholic Danes, who in the Middle Ages partially gained a footing in Dublin and elsewhere for their bishops; but no formal surrender was made by the Church of Ireland to Rome during these ages, save such desultory and spasmodic local efforts as those of the Danes had wrested." [Gubbins, p. 30]

So, we see that the saint is no stranger to controversy, whether in his own time or in ages since. We tend to read into him our own needs and prejudices.

II

Returning to the subject of his true biography, in modern literature there is a variance of at least thirty-odd years in the date of St. Patrick's birth, similarly in the dates of his mission in Ireland and of his death. He was probably born between 385 and 415 C.E. His mission in Ireland likely took place between about 430 and 490 C.E. and was of at least thirty years duration. Some scholars argue that Patrick died in 492–3, and that he came to Ireland only in the year 461; they move his birth forward to around the years 415–6. This is the latterly scheme that, based on the most recent studies, especially Liam de Paor's *Saint Patrick's World*, I lean toward accepting. Due to the complication of Irish annals and careless interpreters and copyists, to say nothing of pious hagiography, the thirty years—at the very least—may well have been lost. The problem may never be resolved.

This chart indicates some of the variety of dating that

various authors have developed, since Bury in 1905, to de Paor in 1993:

AUTHOR	BIRTH DATE	DEATH	LIFE SPAN
J. B. Bury	c. 389	c. 461	72 years
Ludwig Bieler	c. 385	c. 461	76 years
R.P.C. Hanson	c. 390	c. 460	70 years
Liam de Paor	c. 415	c. 493	78 years

Patrick was more or less coeval with some of the greatest Church fathers, among them Pope Celestine I, Pope Leo the Great, St. Augustine of Hippo, and St. Jerome, as well as Pelagius the heresy-monger. During his lifetime, the western empire collapsed at its very center, though Roman influence gained preeminence in the Church partly through the work of Patrick (perhaps despite him) and others on the fringes of the Roman world. At an advanced age (perhaps seventy-five years or more) he died after a mission among the people who came, in later generations, to adopt him as their own patron saint.

The Apostle of Ireland was not a native of that land, but a Roman Briton, born and educated (abortively, inadequately) in the westernmost sector of Britain or Wales. His great-grandfather was Odissus, a deacon; his grandfather, Potitus, was a presbyter, or priest; his father, Calpornius, was a deacon, as well as a decurion, or local magistrate responsible for the collection of taxes. Patrick's mother, according to some sources, was Concessa, possibly a niece of St. Martin of Tours. The family was well-enough-off by any standard, for they lived at a villa, or estate, as Patrick himself writes in the *Confession*. He says in the *Letter* that in later life, whether figuratively or literally, "[I] traded my noble birthright." [*Letter,* ch. 10]

His birthplace appears in the manuscripts as "Bannavem Taberniae." Many historians consider this to be a probable error of copyists, and there are any number of possible interpretations. De Paor follows author Charles Thomas's position that it properly reads "Banna Venta Berniae."

"This would locate Patrick's father's estate," writes de Paor, "at Birdoswald, a short distance west of Luguvallium (Carlisle), on the northern frontier of Roman Britain. There is no certainty about it, however, although the high probability is that Patrick's home was somewhere in the western parts of Britain, open to Irish raids." [de Paor, p. 88] Other authors argue for Dumbarton, Scotland, the western post of the wall originally erected by Agricola, between the Clyde and the Forth, as a barrier against the incursions of the Picts and Scots. In any case, at about age sixteen, Patrick tells us he was taken prisoner by coastal raiders.

For a half century the Bury chronology of events of Patrick's life, as well as geographical situation, was the accepted one. In outline, it is as follows: Patricius, the son of a decurion and deacon, the grandson of a presbyter, having been born in Britain and educated in the Christian faith (though not devout), was growing up on the fringe of an empire that was crumbling in upon itself, when he was taken captive by Irish raiders and taken across the sea to that strange, wild land. Patrick served a master whose name was Miliucc and whose lands were in the part of northern Ireland known as Dalaradia, which somewhat corresponds to today's Ulster. There, he herded pigs on Mount Miss and in the valley of the Braid, in the land of the Picts; he may have changed masters at some point and served in or near the forest of Foclut. He remained homesick and held out the hope of deliverance from bondage—which came to him, miraculously.

He heard a voice that told him, "It is good that you fast, for soon you will return to your own country." [*Confession*, ch. 17] And another night it announced, "Come see, your ship is ready." Patrick escaped, traveled about two hundred miles from his master's house to a port in the vicinity of present-day Wicklow. He knew no one, but the ship of his dreams was there, ready to sail. Patrick was at first denied passage, even after he offered to work for it. Disappointed, he went away from the mariners and prayed. Before he had finished his prayer, one of the crew shouted after him, "Come quickly, for they are calling you." The shipmaster had been persuaded to take him aboard. Legend tells us the ship transported a supply of Irish wolfhounds bound for Nantes or Bordeaux.

Patrick sailed for three days with the heathen crew. The voyage was apparently uneventful. They landed near a desert or a land laid waste by war, and there was no fresh food to be had for twenty-eight days. Starvation threatened, and the shipmaster said to Patrick, "What do you say, Christian? You claim that your God is great and powerful. So why don't you pray for us? For we are in immediate danger of starving; we may not live to see another human being ever again." Patrick, already the missionary, replied, "Trust with all your hearts in the Lord my God—for Him nothing is impossible—so that this day He may send you enough food for your journey until you are satisfied. For He has abundance everywhere." [*Confession*, ch. 19] Immediately some wild pigs appeared on the road, and the starving men killed them and ate and rested for two nights.

Already filled with the Lord, Patrick had another dream, a nightmare in which he was visited by Satan. He struggled, and resisted the devil's temptation with the aid of Christ. There followed another nine days before the wayfarers met up with other men, and Patrick, guided again by a voice in his mind, stayed with his companions (now captors?) two more months.

The ship's crew and their Briton fellow traveler traveled through Gaul and parted in Italy, according to Bury. Then Patrick found a refuge in the monastic community of Honoratus on the Îles de Lérins opposite the cape of Cannes. There he is said to have fallen under the spell of the monastic ideal as an indispensable element in the survival and development of the Christian Church.

Years later Patrick returned home to Britain where his kinsmen greeted him "as a son," and implored him to stay with them. Instead he traveled to Gaul, where he studied at Auxerre, was ordained a deacon by Bishop Amator, and applied himself to the goal of being appointed bishop to the Irish Christians. For when he was home "among my parents" who had joyfully welcomed him and asked him never to leave them again, he had experienced yet another dream:

> There [in Britain] one night I saw a vision of a man, whose name was Victoricus, coming it seemed from Ireland, with countless letters. He gave me one of them, and I read the first words of the letter, which were: "The Voice of the Irish." And as I read aloud the beginning of the letter I imagined that at the same moment I heard their voices—they were those very people who lived hard by the Wood of Foclut, which lies near the Western Sea [where the sun sets]—and thus did they cry out as one: "We ask you, holy boy, come back and walk among us once more."

I was quite brokenhearted and could read no more, and so I woke up. Thanks be to God, after many years the Lord granted to them their desire according to their prayer. [*Confession,* ch. 23]

After the brief mission of Bishop Palladius, which lasted only about one year and ended in his death, Patrick was appointed to succeed him as bishop to the Christians in Ireland in 432. In Ireland he eventually converted the High King, Laoghaire, son of Niall, and triumphed in many confrontations with druidic priests. He established his primary see at Armagh in the north, whence he traveled about the island preaching and baptizing and establishing churches. He organized and disciplined the church in Ireland, established the monastic system, and promoted unity with Rome.

He lived well into old age (possibly his seventies) and lived, semiretired, at Armagh, then at Saul where he wrote his *Confession:* "here he certainly died. . . . The rite of the Eucharist was administered to him at Saul by Bishop Tassach of Raholp, and at Saul he died and was buried. After his death there was no night for twelve days, and folk said that for a whole year the nights were less dark than usually. And other wonders were recorded. Men told how angels kept watch over his body and diffused, as they traveled back to heaven, sweet odors of wine and honey." [Bury, p. 208]

Later writers, basing their conclusions on new translations of the works and new archaeological discoveries in Ireland, differ significantly on issues other than chronology. Few experts today would accept northeastern Ireland as the place of his enslavement (this throws the claims of Mount

Slemish in County Antrim, a still-popular shrine to the saint, into grave doubt). Liam de Paor puts the place of Patrick's Irish captivity in the west of the country in present-day County Mayo, on the western shore of Killala Bay. After all, by his own account, Patrick had to travel about two hundred miles to meet the ship that carried him away from the island. And the voices that he heard in his vision, called him "back" to the forest of Foclut "near the Western Sea." It is likely that he had been there before, and that they knew him—the devout, prayerful shepherd—as a "holy boy."

Similarly, later writers than Bury dispute the entire scenario of Patrick's formation studies in Gaul, whether in Îles de Lérins or Auxerre; also they doubt that he ever went to Rome, and most certainly did not meet either of the two important popes of the age, Celestine I or Leo the Great. Instead, Hanson writes, Patrick was wholly a product of the British Church in both his education and preparation for his ministry, and in the authority of his mission.

In his *Confession* Patrick answers accusations that originate from the Church in Britain; they are very personal, as well as ecclesiastical, charges. In doing so, he provides some details of his activities as bishop among the Irish. "But now, it would be tedious and tiring to relate a detailed accounting of all my works or even parts of them," he avers [ch. 35], yet he cannot help himself: "I am very deeply in God's debt, He who gave me such great grace that so many people were reborn in God through me and afterward confirmed in the Church, and that priests were ordained for them everywhere [ch. 38] . . . This, then, is how the people of Ireland, who had never had any knowledge of God, but until now had cults and worshiped idols and abominations, have lately been turned into a people of the Lord and are called the children of God. Now the sons of the Irish and the daughters of their kings have openly become monks and virgins of Christ." [ch. 41] He "went everywhere" and "baptized many thousands" in his ministry; he was willing to give his life "without hesitation and most gladly for His name," if required.

We read in the *Letter*, a declaration of the excommunication of the *tyrannus* or warlord Coroticus, a nominal Christian, and his soldiers, of Patrick's deep feelings when newly baptized and confirmed Christians are slaughtered and sold into slavery: "What shall I do, O Lord? I am openly despised. Look, all around me Your sheep lie torn and spoiled, and by these very soldiers of Coroticus at his evil orders. Far removed from the love of God is anyone who betrays my newly won Christian into the hands of the Scots and Picts. Voracious wolves have eaten the Lord's flock just when it was increasing in Ireland with tender care. How many sons of Scots kings and daughters of Pictic chiefs have become monks and virgins of Christ—I cannot count their number." [ch. 12]

Note the repetition of the same phraseology in his description of the fruits of his ministry. He was evidently not shy about proclaiming these accomplishments, though he credits God for the strength to be His "fisher and hunter" of souls. [*Confession*, ch. 40]

Clearly, too, Bishop Patrick believed that his mission was the fulfillment of the Christian age, "the last times"— *finem mundi*, the end of the world—bringing as he did the faith to the remotest places of Ireland, "to the remotest parts of the land beyond which there is nothing and nobody, where no one had ever come to baptize, to ordain priests, or to confirm the faithful." [*Confession*, ch. 51]

Patrick's mission was foretold through the prophets and apostles of the Church. He writes:

So whatever happens to me, good or evil, I must accept readily and always give thanks to God, who has taught me to believe in Him always without hesitation. He must have heard my prayer so that I, however unworthy I was, should be granted the ability to undertake this holy and wonderful challenge in these last days; in this way I imitate those who, as the Lord foretold long ago, would preach His gospel as a message to all nations and tribes before the end of the world. So we have seen it happen, and so the prediction has been fulfilled. *Ecce testes sumus, quia Evangelium praedicaum est ubique ubi nemo ultra est.* We ourselves are witnesses that the gospel has been carried unto those places beyond which no one lives. [*Confession,* ch. 34]

Who were these creatures, these people of Ireland, variously described as heathens, pagans, unbelievers, barbarians, and strangers in Patrick's writing and others'? The "Voice of the Irish" had called to him in a dream during the years of his formation in the priesthood. He knew in his heart that he would answer that call, and he wanted to—with all his soul. For he had become one with them, however impossible it would be to become truly one of them. He knew them immediately from his six years' experience among them; we know next to nothing about them.

There is a dearth of information about the place and the people to which Patrick was dispatched as a missionary bishop. Palladius had come before him; perhaps there were others—this we do not know. There is no written record from Patrick's time, except his own: contemporary accounts by and about the Irish simply do not exist. Later writings and native traditions provide vague outlines, but no concrete detail. In recent decades more archaeological evidence has been discovered. The age of Patrick remains essentially "dark."

Liam de Paor, in *Saint Patrick's World: The Christian Culture of Ireland's Apostolic Age*, provides a painstakingly composed portrait of the people whom Patrick hoped to convert and their environment. The preceding centuries had seen increasing cultural influence from Rome, but the legions of the empire had never been employed against the fierce, independent Celts who populated the island. Their society was in flux in the fifth century. Primarily a pastoral and agricultural people, they were ruled by a warrior aristocracy that existed to subjugate and plunder rival tribes; alliances were formed and dissolved, territories conquered and lost. From early historic times (and probably dating to prehistoric ages) there developed a system of local kingships. These clansmen were "primarily captains in war, leaders perhaps of whole migrating peoples winning new settlement land by the sword." [de Paor, p. 27] They frequently adopted the trappings of Roman military-political leaders; earlier traditions dictated that they assume religious leadership, as well.

The landscape presented its own challenge. For thousands of years previous to Patrick's arrival, the island had been inhabited and farmed. However, in Patrick's time "there were no towns or cities. . . . Forests and bogs were extremely extensive, and the numerous undrained lake and river valleys and lowlands created many watery wildernesses in which the traveling stranger would be almost literally at sea. Settlement accordingly was discontinuous, and most inhabited tracts of country would have had something of the character of clearings, in a land where nature was—no doubt red in tooth and claw—but overwhelmingly green." [de Paor, p. 23]

As we have noted, the Roman world considered Hibernia the very ends of the earth, beyond which nothing but sea existed. It was considered as dangerous and exotic as the interior of Africa or the vast spaces of Asia beyond Alexander's long-ago conquests.

Patrick was appointed bishop of the Christians in Ireland, meaning there already existed a Christian population, however small and probably scattered throughout the island. Many, if not most, of these Christians were captives from Irish raids—just as Patrick himself had been—or the descendants of such captives. It is probable that they were originally Roman Britons—as was Patrick. Thus the British Church, and indirectly the Church of Rome, gained a tentative, tenuous foothold on the wild, distant island of Hibernia. As much as he—and presumably others—wanted it, this was no plum assignment: a missionary diocese that was dangerous and harsh, with a fragile and immature faith community that had long been without proper supervision.

Again, de Paor illuminates the situation Patrick faced:

Most of what we can guess about pre-Christian Ireland suggests a tissue of magical practices and rituals, the observation of omens, the use of spells and incantatory formulas and the avoidance of unlucky actions. Christian teaching had to find a way through a labyrinth of fear, superstitious observances and worship (ultimately of the elements of nature)—which included some form of sun worship. The first preachers of the gospel show a particular concern to emphasize God's power over the sun, the sky, the wind and all such elemental forces. It is not surprising that often in popular belief Christian teaching was overwhelmed by the pagan tradition, or that in the storytelling the very missionaries themselves disappear beneath a web of old anecdotes originally told about the local divinities who had preceded them. [de Paor, p. 29]

The kings and druids were by their very nature hostile to Patrick's mission. At the same time, Patrick apparently encountered a willing and generous people who showed their gratitude to him with offers of gifts, which he, on principle, refused. (He was compelled to point this out in his defense against clerical accusations in Britain.) It was probably difficult to turn away the heartfelt expressions of his converts; he gave much and yet expected nothing in return but their faith. This they gave in great numbers and heartfelt sincerity. And herein lies his primary legacy— apart from the affection in which the Irish people still hold him: the once-tenuous faith tradition of the early Church flowered so rapidly and deeply that Ireland is today, fifteen hundred years later, the "most Catholic" country on earth thanks to his evangelizing zeal.

We must remember that he chose to live in this distant and alien but not unfamiliar (to him) land as a demonstration of his commitment to Christ. His mission took him back to the site of his captivity and enslavement, and he vowed never to leave the Irish people again, as long as he lived. To the "heathens" who were his former captors, he brought the ultimate and most precious gift: the love of God.

III

Let us now consider, in brief, some of the legendary aspects of Patrick's story, for purposes of rounding out our portrait and acknowledging that these tales have shaped the image and meaning of the great saint that survives into our time.

For example, there is the story of Benignus from the Book of Armagh, which takes place early in Patrick's mission.

Patrick and his entourage of priests and workers sailed up the mouth of the River Boyne, left their boats under guard, and proceeded on foot to convert the locals. They started, and immediately succeeded, with the house of an Irish chieftain, Seschnen.

The party then retired for the evening. One of the children of the household, a little boy, Benin, who had listened to Patrick's preaching of the gospel, cast fragrant flowers over the sleeping St. Patrick, despite his parents' remonstrations. In the morning when the saint was getting into his chariot, and had one foot in and the other on the ground, the child held his foot tightly in both hands, and cried, "Let me go with Patrick, my true father!" The boy was allowed to join the bishop's party, was instructed and baptized by Patrick, and became his constant companion.

In later years, under the name of Benignus, the worshipful boy became Patrick's successor at Armagh.

In the legendary lives of the saint, two men played especially important roles in Patrick's life in Ireland: Miliucc, his master during his period of enslavement, and Laoghaire, the druid king of Tara, son of Niall, the chief of the Irish raiding party that had abducted him in the first place (unless, as some versions have it, Niall had died, at the hands of his countrymen, shortly before Patrick was taken). Fire also played an important role in the lives of these three men, and in all cases, the overcoming of fire is a clear symbol of the overcoming of the ego, of hubris; it is a symbol of humility. Fire can reduce the mightiest hero or most magnificent home to ashes, just as it can give unwonted power to an otherwise powerless person.

In the case of Miliucc, legend has it that the special qualities of Patrick so impressed the pagan chieftain of northern Dalaradia that he came to think the unthinkable: that he was unworthy of being master to such as Patrick. The young Patrick's devotion to God—a God about whom Patrick was as yet unclear, a God he was later to accept wholly through the doctrine of the Church—in the form of prayer and kindness shook the foundations of Miliucc's belief in his right to enslave all whom he had captured or bought for the purpose. Miliucc must have, like others of his clan, watched in amazement as Patrick arose in the morning to pray, standing in the open air, his arms raised heavenward, braving rain, or cold, or snow, or heat.

Patrick was no less compassionate to his master after he escaped. He eventually returned to England and, with the help of his family, declared his freedom. But he insisted on paying homage to his former master and went to see him to purchase his freedom. Miliucc heard of the approaching bishop and was consumed with terror.

Was he fearful that Patrick was coming to exact vengeance for his servitude? He may have had some such fears, but he knew the lad better; Patrick's design was not revenge. Was he coming to lord over the local chieftain, perhaps even to enslave him? Doubtful. Miliucc was perhaps more concerned about simply the confrontation, of having to stare directly into the face of his own defeated ego. He had dared to claim mastery over such a man as Patrick. The prospect of being so humbled was too much, and Miliucc immolated himself before Patrick arrived.

The bishop was saddened by the death of his old master, saddened by Miliucc's succumbing to the deadly sin of pride. It was a lesson for Patrick of the power of his mission and of the value and importance of humility.

The druid seers along the River Boyne had foretold of the coming of an "adze-head"—a Briton—who would triumph over their religion. Some years earlier, the first bishop sent among the Christian believers in Ireland, Palladius, had mysteriously—or perhaps not so mysteriously—died before firmly establishing his episcopate. Ruling the people from the ancient capital of Tara was the warrior-king Laoghaire; this ruler was well aware of the failure of the first bishop. He knew, too, that the new man, Patrick, had been abducted in a long-ago raid by his father and that Patrick had returned and vanquished his old master.

It seems Laoghaire was fascinated by Patrick, aware that the newly consecrated bishop had powerful gifts of persuasion, and that he was every bit a match for the king's own miracle worker, Lucat Moel. The challenge to Laoghaire's supreme authority was quick and direct: immediately upon his arrival in the area on the eve of the Christian feast of Easter, without asking or awaiting permission, Patrick lit a paschal fire on a hillside visible from Tara. This defiance of the king's and the druids' authority was a capital crime. The various legends tell that Patrick was brought before the king and an explanation was demanded by the sword-wielding viscount, Lochru. Patrick miraculously lifted the warrior into the air, then let him drop to the earth, disabling (possibly killing) him.

From this point on, the druids feared and respected Patrick; Laoghaire then tested the bishop at every opportunity, pitting his druid magicians against Patrick many times. There grew between the two men a respect and a deference, perhaps even an admiration. Laoghaire himself would never convert to Christianity, nor accept Patrick as his confessor, but the king's wives and all their sons and daughters did. In spite of his victories, however, and after his first challenge, Patrick never failed to show Laoghaire the respect due him as king. Patrick the bishop and former slave respected his own place within God's scheme—as he understood it.

The *Tripartite Life of St. Patrick*, in various nineteenth-century translations—including Todd's, in his famous and controversial biography, and William Maunsell Hennessy's, printed in the *Life* by M. F. Cusack [pp. 404–408]—relates a pivotal, if apocryphal tale of the evangelizing bishop. This "dialogue" with two daughters of the supposed high king of Ireland was said to have taken place near Cruachan, now Rathcroghan in County Roscommon, the ancient residence of the kings of Connaught.

Patrick had been about the country establishing churches with his ever-expanding entourage of priests and assistants when he went to wash himself at the well (*ad fontem*) called Clebach on the east side of the mountain. There, at sunrise, he and his party sat, dressed in white with books in hand. "The virgins [Laoghaire MacNeill's two daughters, Ethne the Fair (*alba*) and Fidelma the Red (*rufa*)] came early to the well, to wash, after the manner of women, and they found near the well a synod of clerics with Patrick. They wondered at the appearance of these men, and supposed them to be Duine Sidhe (the men of *sidhe*, or fairies), or gods of the earth, or phantoms." [Cusack, p. 404]

The young women questioned Patrick and the men:

"Who are you? When came you? And where are you from? Are you gods?"

Patrick replied, "It would be better for you to believe in our true God than to ask regarding our race."

The first virgin said, "Who is your God? Where dwells your God—in heaven or in earth? Is he under the earth or on the earth or in the sea or in the rivers or in hills or in valleys? What is his nature? Has your God sons and daughters? Has he gold and silver? Is there a profusion of every good in his kingdom? Is he beautiful? Have many men fostered his Son? Are his daughters beautiful and dear to the men of the world? Is he young or old? Or is he ever-living? Tell us plainly how we shall see him, and how is he to be loved and how is he to be found?"

St. Patrick, full of the Holy Spirit, responded, "Our God is the God of all men, the God of heaven and earth, the God of the seas and rivers, the God of the sun and moon and all the other planets and stars. He is the God of the high mountains and low valleys, the God who is above heaven, in heaven, and under heaven. He has a mansion in heaven, in the earth and the sea, and all things that are in them.

"He inspires all things. He quickens all things. He is over all things. He sustains all things. He gives light to the sun, and He illuminates the night by sharing his brightness with the moon. He has made springs in the dry ground and placed dry islands in the sea and appointed stars to serve the greater lights.

"He has a son, coeternal and coequal with Himself. The Son is not younger than the Father, nor is the Father older than the Son. And the Holy Spirit breathes in them both. The Father, the Son, and the Holy Spirit are not divided. But I desire to unite you to the Son of the heavenly King, for you are daughters of an earthly king."

The daughters said, as with one mouth and one heart, "Teach us how we may believe in the heavenly King. Show us how we may see Him face to face. Teach us, and we will do whatever you tell us to do."

Patrick replied, "Do you believe that through baptism the sin of your mother and father shall be put aside?"

They answered, "We believe."

"Do you believe in repentance after sin?"

"Yes, we believe."

"Do you believe in life after death? Do you believe in the resurrection at the Day of Judgment?"

"We believe."

"Do you believe in the unity of the Church?"

Again they answered, "We believe."

Then they were baptized, and Patrick blessed a white veil to put upon their heads. And they asked to see the face of Christ. The saint said to them, "You cannot see the face of Christ, except that you first taste of death, and unless you first receive the body of Christ and His blood."

The king's daughters said, "Give us the Holy Communion so that we may behold the One you have prophesied." So they received the Eucharist and fell asleep and died.

Patrick's priests laid the two maidens on a single bed, covered them with garments, and their friends made great lamentation and weeping over them. The druids came and confronted Patrick over his conversion of the young women and their being taken to heaven. The magus Caplit came, grieving over the second daughter, whom he had fostered. Patrick preached to him, and Caplit believed, and he cut off his hair.

The other druid, Caplit's brother Mael, came and said, "My brother has believed in you, but it shall not serve nor strengthen him for I will lead him back to paganism."

He spoke harsh, insulting words to Patrick, but Patrick preached to him and converted him to the repentance of God. Patrick shaved him, too, replacing the druidical tonsure that was a symbol of damnation with a Christian tonsure. From this event came the proverb, "Mael is bald like Caplit," for together they believed in God.

The days of mourning for the king's two daughters ended, and they were buried near the well of Clebach where they first met Patrick; and they made a circular ditch (ferta) in the custom of the Scotic people, creating a reliquary for the remains of the virgins. There the bones of the holy virgins are destined to lie forever.

Patrick erected an earthen church in that place.

These conversions reflect the primary purpose of Patrick's mission. In addition, there are hundreds of miracle tales that cling like barnacles to the underside of the saint's life. Cheeses, curds, bells, lepers, fire—all are employed in the making of these supposed magic tricks. Sometimes there are morals attached to the miracle tales, but often the stunts stand on their own as "proof" of divine endorsement of Patrick's mission. And woe be unto any poor druid who dared to defy the pyrotechnical missionary!

When St. Patrick was departing the coast of Britain to come over to Ireland on his mission, just as his ship had cast off from the shore, a poor leprous man came on the beach and begged earnestly to be taken on board. Patrick was willing to put back and take him aboard, but the crew refused, and the small fleet of ships moved on. The poor leper loudly continued his entreaties, whereupon Patrick took his altar stone (which in the old writings is called "the stone altar") and cast it out on the water within reach of the leper. Patrick ordered him to sit on it and be quiet. This the leper did, and immediately the stone moved, following the ship throughout its course until they reached the harbor of Wicklow, where the leper was one of the first to land.

There the saint again took possession of his "stone altar." This stone is spoken of as an altar in the text of this prophecy, and with the promise that as long as it lives in Ireland, Patrick's children in Christ will live in his doctrine. It is not improbable that there was an ancient legend, which is now forgotten, of the history of this stone before Patrick consecrated it to holy purposes. [Cusack, pp. 108–109]

Several miracles are related in various *Lives* as having happened while he was still a child. On one occasion a nearby house where his "nurse" lived was flooded, and since the fire was extinguished, no food could be cooked. The child had asked for food, but the nurse replied that they must have a fire kindled before she could feed him. St. Patrick then went to a part of the house that the water had not yet reached. There he dipped his fingers in some water, and as five drops fell from his five fingers they were miraculously changed into sparks of fire.

On another occasion, when playing with his little companions in the wintertime, he brought to his nurse (presumably the same lucky lady) an armful of ice sheets. The intense cold of a severe winter had probably caused some difficulty in procuring firewood, and the nurse exclaimed that it would be better if he had brought her some fagots to burn. The boy replied that it was easy for fire to prevail over water, if God willed that it should be so. Then, casting the ice upon the fire, he made the sign of the cross and breathed over it. As he did, long streams of flame burst forth, which gave light and heat to the room. Those who surrounded this marvelous fire looked and wondered, for they also beheld flames of light issuing forth from the boy-saint's face.

It would appear that St. Patrick, as a boy, had been employed in tending sheep before his enforced servitude. Once, while he and his sister were thus engaged, the lambs came suddenly to their mothers, and Patrick hastened with his sister to drive them away. As they ran, the little girl fell, and to all appearances she had received a fatal blow; the young saint at once raised her up and made the sign of the cross on her over the wound, which was instantly healed. Only the "white wound" remained to testify to the miracle.

Once, also, their flock was attacked by a wolf, who carried off a sheep. The (seemingly ever-present) nurse reproached Patrick for his neglect in permitting this, but on the following day the wolf appeared again and brought back the sheep with him. This good woman then wished never to leave her charge, and well she might be faithful to him, when she saw him thus "magnified by God" in prodigies and miracles. At one time Patrick restored to life five cows who had been killed by a vicious cow; at another time, when he went to some assembly with his nurse and guardian, the latter fell dead, but was restored to life by the prayers of St. Patrick.

On yet another occasion, his nurse reproached him because he did not bring home supplies of wild honey as other boys did, and Patrick returned to the well, filled his bucket with water, and at once it was changed into the purest honey. Again, when a tribute of curds and butter was required, and there was none to supply the demand, St. Patrick made curds and butter of the snow. [Cusack, pp. 118–120]

My favorite miracle tale is matter-of-factly recorded in the *Tripartite Life*. And here is my favorite translation, the one by Hennessy:

They came then to a place called Dal-in-Buinne [near modern-day Belfast], where he, Patrick, prayed and sat; and Sechnall [Secundinus] afterwards sang the remainder of the hymn [his poetic eulogy of praise that he reluctantly shared with the saint]; and Patrick heard his name and thereupon thanked him. Three pieces of cheese, and butter, were brought up to him from a religious couple named Berach and Brig. "Here is for the young men," said the woman. "Good," said Patrick. A druid came there, whose name was Gall-drui [meaning foreign druid], who said, "I will believe in you if you convert the pieces of cheese into stones," which God performed through Patrick. "Again convert them into cheese." Patrick did. "Convert them into stones again." Patrick again did it. "Convert them again." But Patrick said, "No, but they will be as they are, in commemoration, until the servant of God, who is Dieuill of Ernaidhe [the future Abbot of Louth, c. 700 C.E.], shall come here." The druid magus promptly believed.

Patrick flung his little bell under a dense bush there. A birch grew through its handle. This it was that Dieuill found, the *betechan*, Patrick's bell—a little iron bell—which is in the Ernaidhe of Dieuill. And two of the stones made of the cheese are there; the third one was, moreover, carried by Dieuill to Lugmagh, when he was abbot there. It is today in Gort-Conaidh. [Cusack, p. 494–495]

One of the later accretions of myth and legend that adheres to the saint's modern identity is St. Patrick's Purgatory. Legend places Patrick at a cave on an island in Lough Derg where he "retired" at some point in his life; from inside the cave he stepped directly into purgatory, the nether state for sinners who require further purgation of their moral failings before being admitted to heaven.

St. Patrick's Purgatory was one of the most enduring religious myths of the Middle Ages, as author Shane Leslie described it, "the medieval rumor which terrified travelers, awed the greatest criminals, attracted the boldest of knight errantry, puzzled the theologian, englamoured Ireland, haunted Europe, influenced the current view and doctrines of Purgatory, and not least inspired Dante." [Leslie, p. 19] Today pilgrims still go to the "Purgatory" on Station Island in Lough Derg, a long, snaky lake in west-central Ireland north of Limerick. But these are spiritual seekers who experience a cleansing ritual of fasting, abstinence, and prayer; they are not adventurers, knights-errant, or mystics who were once said to have glimpsed sinners and saints in a dreadful preview of the afterlife.

The earliest *Lives* contain no mention of the cave on Saints Island—a neighbor of Station Island—in which St. Patrick was granted this vision of purgatory. The origin of the tradition has been traced to the twelfth century author Henry of Saltrey, an Anglo-Norman Cistercian monk who published *Tractatus de Purgatorio S. Patricii*. In this popular work was a tale, which Henry said he learned from a fellow monk named Gilbert. From this point, for several centuries, the myth spawned narratives, songs, poems, prayers, and other fantastic accounts of pilgrims who went to the cave where God had supposedly revealed purgatory to St. Patrick.

Through a later period of destruction under Protestant church leaders, in the seventeenth century, the devotion to Patrick and at least the place itself survived. Now there is a basilica and visitor center that receives tens of thousands of pilgrims annually for a three-day regime of fasting, vigils, and stations. There is no official church teaching, no accepted biographical evidence, and no mention in his own writings that Patrick was granted a vision of that place of purgation between heaven and hell.

♣

As much fun as these adventures are, a reality check is necessary here. Paul Gallico, in his magnificent 1958 book, brings us back to earth:

> On page after page of legend, miracle story, and manuscript buried in monastery libraries you will find that other Patrick who never existed wandering about Ireland, bringing the promise of the Gospels but also working much mischief upon pagans who, if not wholly innocent, were, to say the least, bewildered by this short-tempered man who went cursing and punishing and death-dealing across the length and breadth of their land, with a vindictiveness that is little short of startling. Nothing escaped his short temper and vengefulness....

Occasionally a spark of humor illuminates the grim pro-
cession of church foundings, curses, rewards, punish-
ments, foiling of attempted ambushes and poison plots,
bitter-bit stories and the like. [Gallico, pp. 101–102]

Are these characteristics more reflective of the writers
and preservers—monks, priests, copyists—than of Patrick
himself? One thinks so.

IV

Early in his papacy, John Paul II made an apostolic
trip to Ireland (September 29 to October 1, 1979) where
he frequently invoked Patrick's heritage and explicitly proclaimed the saint's primacy and patronage of the Irish
Church. At Armagh, the pope quoted early records that
"attest" that Palladius was sent to Ireland by Pope Celestine I and that Patrick succeeded Palladius, and was "confirmed in the faith" by Pope Leo the Great. In Galway, he
reminded the faithful, "Today, for the first time since St.
Patrick preached the faith to the Irish, the Successor of
Peter comes from Rome and sets foot on Irish soil."

The Holy Father met a group of seminarians at St.
Patrick's College at Maynooth on October 1. He addressed
them on the subject of "Dedication to Christ and His
Word," as follows:

Dear brothers and sons in our Lord Jesus Christ,

You have a very special place in my heart and in the
heart of the Church. During my visit to Maynooth I
wanted to be alone with you, even though it could be
for only a few moments.

I have many things I would tell you—things that I

have been saying about the life of seminarians and about seminaries all during the first year of my pontificate.

In particular I would like to speak again about the Word of God: about how you are called to hear and guard and do the Word of God. And about how you are to base your entire lives and ministry upon the Word of God, just as it is transmitted by the Church, just as it is expounded by the Magisterium, just as it has been understood throughout the history of the Church by the faithful guided by the Holy Spirit: *semper et ubique et ab omnibus* [always and everywhere and from all people].

The Word of God is the great treasure of your lives. Through the Word of God you will come to a deep knowledge of the mystery of Jesus Christ, Son of God and Son of Mary: Jesus Christ, the High Priest of the New Testament and the Savior of the world.

The Word of God is worthy of all your efforts. To embrace it in its purity and integrity, and to spread it by word and example is a great mission. And this is your mission, today and tomorrow and for the rest of your lives.

As you pursue your vocation—a vocation so intimately related to the Word of God, I wish to recall to you one simple but important lesson taken from the life of St. Patrick, and it is this: in the history of evangelization, the destiny of an entire people—your people—was radically affected for time and eternity because of the fidelity with which St. Patrick embraced and proclaimed the Word of God, and by reason of the fidelity with which St. Patrick pursued his call to the end.

What I really want you to realize is this: that God counts on you: that He makes His plans, in a way, depends on your free collaboration, on the oblation of your lives, and on the generosity with which you follow the inspirations of the Holy Spirit in the depths of your hearts.

The Catholic faith of Ireland today was linked, in God's plan, to the fidelity of Patrick. And tomorrow, yes, tomorrow some part of God's plan will be linked to your fidelity—to the fervor with which you say yes to God's Word in your lives.

Today Jesus Christ is making this appeal to you through me: the appeal for fidelity. In prayer you will see more and more every day what I mean and what the implications of this call are. By God's grace you will understand more and more every day how God requires and accepts your fidelity as a condition for the supernatural effectiveness of all your activity. The supreme expression of fidelity will come with your irrevocable and total self-giving in union with Jesus Christ to His Father. And may our blessed Mother Mary help you make this gift acceptable.

Remember St. Patrick. Remember what the fidelity of just one man has meant for Ireland and the world. Yes, dear sons and brothers, fidelity to Jesus Christ and to His Word makes all the difference in the world. Let us therefore look up to Jesus, who is for all time the faithful witness of the Father. [John Paul II, pp. 121–125]

I cannot imagine a more forthright papal endorsement of the message of the ancient saint. Pope John Paul II finds the immediate relevance of Patrick's vocation and his steadfastness to the Church's struggle to recruit and train more priests. We can apply the same characteristics to our lives as lay men and women. Patrick, like St. Paul, is a direct, prophetic link between the gospel and the average Christian.

Did he establish Armagh as the primatial see of Ireland? It is possible. Did he retire there, or die there? That is more questionable.

As Hanson writes, "His life ends as far as we are concerned in total darkness lit only by the will-o'-the-wisp of later legend." [Hanson, *Life and Writings,* p. 55]

HUMILITY

I am Patrick, a sinner, the most unlearned [i.e., rustic, unschooled] and least of all the faithful, and utterly despised by many. My father was a certain man named Calpornius, a deacon, son of the late Potitus, a presbyter, who was in the town of Bannaventa Berniae. He had a small estate nearby. There I was captured and made a slave. I was not even sixteen years old. I was ignorant of the true Lord, and so I was led to Ireland in captivity with many thousands of others, who deserved this fate, because we cut ourselves off from God, because we did not keep His commandments, because we were disobedient to our priests who admonished us about our salvation.

And so the Lord revealed to us His wrath and indignation and scattered us among many nations [heathen tribes], even unto the farthest ends of the earth, where I am now, in my lonely insignificance, among strangers.

Then the Lord opened my mind and senses to the nature of my unbelief so that I may—however late—remember my sins and turn with all my heart to the Lord my God. He turned His attention to my abject humility [insignificance] and took pity on my youth and ignorance. He watched over me and protected me before I knew Him and before I was wise enough to distinguish between good and evil. He strengthened and comforted me as a father consoles a son.

[CONFESSION, CH. 1–2]

Commentary

When Patrick wrote the first words of his *Confession*—his spiritual autobiography and defense against clerical accusers—he was an elderly, experienced evangelist under fire from the Catholic Church hierarchy in his homeland, Britain. His words were designed to teach, more than to unburden himself; his was not an age of therapeutic self-revelation. His story can help us when we, like Patrick, man and boy, find ourselves embedded in burdensome complexities—relationships, responsibilities, mental and spiritual fatigue—that we face every day.

Magonus Sucatus Patricius began life as the son of a landed family in far western Britain. His father was a Roman citizen and he was given a Roman name. We sense that young Patricius was not one to remain in the village and tend to his studies. He was from his youth a lover of nature, and he accepts the charge of being "rustic"—one of the criticisms lodged against him by enemies among the British clergy—with some ironic pride. We can sense the alienation the young man felt from his earthly father—the most natural of things in human relationships.

Here is the insight that begins Patrick's journey: that God's love for him is the love of a father for a son. Though the son is not always aware of the father, though he is un-mindful of the admonishments offered in His name, though he be estranged and tempest-tossed to foreign shores, he is aware that his rescue—his salvation—came about only be-cause his Heavenly Father watched over him and protected him. Patrick, though, feels deeply unworthy of this Father's love. Six years of hard servitude in northern Ireland saw him a literal shepherd (or cowherd, or perhaps swineherd) imbibing the beauty of the countryside and becoming in-toxicated with the presence of God that he felt in the natu-ral surroundings and in the hearts of the people he met. The connection Patrick felt—and eventually embodied—between the natural beauty of the land and the open, lov-ing, and generous hearts of its people, was the beginning of his journey to being not merely a missionary to Ireland, but its apostle and patron saint.

It seems that Patrick achieved a laudable balance be-tween the extremes of self-righteousness and abject guilt (that is, self-destruction). That balance is humility, which allowed him to place his feet on the path that God ordained for him and veer not one way or the other from that path. He was, in fact, clothed in righteousness, but did not lord it over others. Patrick also was stricken with guilt over past conduct and tasks undone, but did not allow that feeling to paralyze him into inaction. He was a man of action always with a clear vision of the eternal.

Of course, he did not operate alone or make the rules himself. Patrick did not found a religious movement, but was a pious follower of a tradition that had been four cen-turies in development. There was a hierarchy in place: pope, bishops, priests and deacons, acolytes, laymen. He strove to find his rightful place in that system—and he did. However, he always felt less than adequate in his person, however strongly he held his faith. He was less educated, clearly. But, at an even deeper level, he understood that as a human being he was unworthy of the blessings that his God had bestowed upon him. He "deserved" to be enslaved, because as a youth he had turned from the commandments and God's earthly representatives, the clergy. So had many others.

Patrick took himself to task more than he berated anyone else. This is Patrick: self-abasing to an almost embarrassing degree. I find it difficult not to wince as he repeatedly puts himself down in the eyes of his fellow Churchmen: "utterly despised by many."

Patrick credits God directly with opening his heart, mind, and senses to the truth of His existence. It is not an act of human will but a gift, perhaps undeserved, from a divine force that is otherwise incomprehensible to the recipient. He felt that he was, in fact, among the least deserving of God's grace. Thus his exile—one could say exiles, since he, like Aeneas or Odysseus, spent much of his life wandering far from his original home on the coast of Britain—was part of a providential scheme over which he had no control; his role was to respond to each challenge in a way pleasing to God.

He does not put himself above any man, even in his role of bishop.

Patrick's example is a powerful one. Blessed with many things, denied many others, he soldiered on through slavery, wandering, a difficult education, mission, opposition, and infirm old age. God most assuredly touched this man of the ancient world with the fire of faith and humility that burdened through the centuries down to our own day. Yet, he did not seek this uniqueness that we attribute to him, for he called himself the "least" and most "despised." It is no accident that Patrick's stark admission of humility comes in the first sentence of his life story. He believed his own position was lowly and unworthy; he saw himself as a servant of God and his fellows in the quest for salvation in Christ Jesus.

Contemplation

Am I falsely modest; do I assume an outward humility merely as a way of masking my ego? Am I "too big for my britches" as a way of coping with an uncomfortable situation? Or am I honest and realistic about where I stand in the eyes of God and my fellows? Why do I not always recognize and humbly accept God's gifts in my life? What is the true meaning of humility? How can humility become a part of my life?

Can I not learn that all the hardships I face—rejection, illness, addiction, misunderstanding, unjust treatment—are but steps along the path that requires of me only that I put one foot in front of the other?

There are many examples in my life that I may learn from: a father's long years of labor to support a large family with no thought to fame or recognition, no thought to personal comfort; likewise, a mother's denial of career or material gratification for the sake of her children and her husband; a friend who has lived in a sickbed for years waiting for a call or a visit from me that takes months to arrive, yet who responds joyfully and with gratitude and not with harsh judgment; the coworker who one day is not in the next-door office because she has been fired to make way for a hotshot executive with a grander title and portfolio; the schoolchild seeking my help with homework that is "over my head." These are the tablets upon which God writes messages for me: take no material advantage for granted; nurture gratitude as a gorgeous flowering plant that blooms every day of the year; this, too (the good and the ill), shall pass.

St. Patrick labored on through good times and bad, meeting the challenges of his enemies and the natural environment and his own limitations. He presented to the world a face of confidence and a positive message of love and faith. When Miliucc killed himself, when Laoghaire's minions cursed him, when he stepped into any inhospitable situation, Patrick relied upon God for strength and direction. He knew that the power to perform miracles of evangelization did not come from himself. His education, his mission, his very survival against incredible odds were gifts from the Father.

Despite himself, he achieved a position in history that compares to Moses and St. Paul; yet he did not seek this specialness that we attribute to him, for he calls himself the "least" and most "despised." And he believed that his own position was lowly and unworthy. Humility became for Patrick a watchword and a way of life.

Humility is not so much the opposite of pride as it is a clear understanding of my daily reality. Humility does not mean humiliation or helplessness or abasement. It does not mean I will allow another person to walk all over me. To possess true humility means that I accept God's gifts and life's trials with the grace God also offers so freely to me as an unworthy, prodigal son or daughter.

Humility is often a tug-and-pull affair: on the one hand, often I have every right and reason for pride in my family or my own accomplishments or my crystal-pure motives (that is, I mean well, don't I?); on the other hand, was I not wrong or stupid to have done such a thing, or they don't really like me at all (nor do I value myself, in this state of mind). Either extreme can be destructive. A middle ground is the way for me.

Bill W., the founder of Alcoholics Anonymous, a spiritual movement based on one person helping another, with reliance on God or a "Higher Power" in the process, wrote on this subject, in his book *As Bill Sees It*: "Absolute humility would consist of a state of complete freedom from myself, freedom from all the claims that my defects of character now lay so heavily upon me. Perfect humility would be a full willingness, in all times and places, to find and to do the will of God." [p. 106]

Prayer

Father, I pray that you may grant me the ability to be what You created me to be: no greater, no smaller, no better nor worse—that I may accept my right size and station in the world while being of humble and willing service to others in my life. Grant me the freedom from ego and false pride that blocks me in relationships with others to whom I would be of help. God the Father, hear my prayer.

IMPERFECTION

Even though I am imperfect in so many aspects of my life, nevertheless I wish that my brethren and my family should know what sort of person I am, so that they may clearly understand my heart and soul's desire [my mettle].

I know very well the testimony of my Lord, who in the psalm plainly teaches: "You will destroy those who speak lies." And again He declares: "The mouth that lies kills a man's soul." And the same Lord says in the Gospel: "Every idle word that people shall speak, they will be asked to account for it on the day of judgment."

So I cannot be unaware of these Gospel warnings. Indeed, I am filled with fear and trembling of such a sentence on that day, when no one will be able to escape or hide; but all of us, without exception, shall be called to own up to even our smallest sins before the tribunal of Our Lord Jesus Christ, the Son of the Father.

Because of this I have for a long time intended to write, but *until now have hesitated; for I was afraid of exposing myself to the talk [criticism] of men, because I have not gotten a proper education like the others who thoroughly and easily absorbed both the law and the sacred Scripture, and never had to change from the language of their childhood. Instead, they were able to polish it and make it more perfect. Whereas in my case, what I write or speak must be translated into a tongue that is still foreign to me; this can be easily proved from the flavor of my writing, which reveals how little instruction and training I have had in the art of rhetoric. As the Scripture says, "By his tongue [language] the wise man will be known—as will understanding and knowledge and truth."*

[*CONFESSION*, CH. 6–9]

Commentary

Another of Patrick's core virtues, as expressed in his own words, was his acceptance of his manifest imperfections—as well as his Imperfection, writ large. This state was, for him, a matter of fact and a matter for rejoicing. His frankness is disarming here as in so much of his writing: he wishes us to know just what sort of person he is, and he knows that this person falls far short of the ideal standards of the Roman world and the Christian Church.

The Church of saints Augustine of Hippo and Jerome, later of St. Thomas Aquinas and the modern fathers (since the first Vatican Council), has taught us that perfection is in fact achievable through faith and communion with Christ. Not in this world, mind you, but in the next—with the added kicker that it is *forever*, through all eternity. Frankly, that is too much for many human (i.e., limited and imperfect) minds to grapple with, both in terms of the state of perfection itself and the time frame involved: forever and *ever*?

At some time in his youth—perhaps at age fifteen, as specified in the *Confession*, though not corroborated in other, later biographical sources—Sucatus committed a terrible mortal sin. What was it? Theft? Murder? Adultery? Rape? False witness against another? We can only conjecture. The Roman garrison town near where Patrick's family's estate lay probably was an occasion for any type or degree of sin for a hot-blooded young Briton. The empire brought law and social order, education and literature to the borders of the known western world. (Britain was at this time the farthest northwestern extent of Roman influence; Ireland was beyond the Roman ken.)

The empire also sowed corruption and vice, violence and slavery in its wake. And in the early fifth century C.E., it was teetering on the brink of its own precipitous and irrevocable decline: "A mighty, monstrous, cruel and splendid civilization was breaking. Outlying parts offered easy plunder to the young, untamed races beyond Rome's olden pale." [De Blácam, *Gentle Ireland*, p. 35] In this fringe of imperial decadence, distant from the notorious capital yet distinctly a product thereof, we might assume that the boy fell victim to a powerful temptation. Let us leave it unnamed, but assume that it was a heinous act.

In time, Patrick confessed his sin of unsurpassed wickedness (at least in his mind) and went on to become an ordained deacon of the Church, and later was consecrated as bishop. At some point later in his ecclesiastical career, that old sin came back to haunt him: a close friend and priest, to whom he had confessed, revealed the sin to a synod of the British Church sitting in judgment of Patrick. By this time, the ardent apostle had made enemies; they sought, and found, ammunition to discredit him. Patrick's *Confession* is in large measure a response to this attack. But in defending himself, he readily admits to this sin and others, to imperfection and unworthiness in the sight of God and man.

> Patrick's weaknesses were those of the modern self-made man. He was sensitive to criticism; he was inclined to be scornful of men of book learning, considering what he had accomplished with so little of it, and he was disposed to be suspicious and apparently accepted things on hearsay. The bitterest blow of his life, his betrayal at the hands of his dearest friend, was reported to him at second, and perhaps even third hand, and believed. If the report was untrue—and there is a considerable possibility that it might have been—no man ever suffered more than Patrick for this fault.
>
> Yet in one important factor Patrick differed from the modern success, the fellow who has raised himself aloft by his bootstraps. All of the credit for his achievements he ascribes to God. [Gallico, pp. 131–132]

Further, Patrick does not fall into our culture of blame, for, although he vigorously defends himself from numerous charges of illegality and immorality, he nowhere blames any other person for his faults or sinful actions. Throughout the *Confession* he emphasizes his own myriad shortcomings and praises God for His tolerance of such an imperfect servant.

Specifically, Patrick faults his inability to express himself adequately in Latin. He uses the vulgar, or spoken, form of Latin in his writings, not the elevated rhetoric of the poets and politicians who employ language for effect.

He is struggling to tell the truth as he knows it to an audience not easy to sway.

He is aware, too, that the day of judgment is at hand, according to the accepted teachings of his Church, and his close reading of Scripture. While no scholar himself, Patrick studied his Bible and became intimately acquainted with the prophecies of the ancient prophets, as well as St. Paul's admonitions to the far-flung, young Christian communities of the Mediterranean world. He was living proof, by the nature of his ministry to the outpost of humanity at the end of the known world, that the gospel message had penetrated as far as it could, and that his Savior would soon call him, and his converts, to account.

Patrick will bring to the tribunal of Christ a bundle of Patrician imperfections: a history of sin, halting speech, an uncultivated mind, personal ambition and pride, powerful anger, self-justification, fear. He is very unlike others whom he cites in chapter 9 of the *Confession*: those who have perfected the arts of rhetoric and persuasion, who have mastered language, who have easily absorbed the legal and scriptural underpinnings of the Church. These are men, presumably, who will "go far," who are rising stars in the sight of God. Patrick lags behind them. He has been held back by circumstance, perhaps by temperament.

If, as seems apparent, the *Confession* is a defense against certain unspecified charges from Britain, Patrick is under intense pressure at a time in his life when, perhaps, he has retired or semiretired from active ministry. He may be very old at this time; he reminds the reader that this is his testimony before he dies. So he may be squaring earthly accounts before facing the ultimate accounting.

There is a hesitation, an ambivalence, nonetheless in

his testimony. It is as if he expects not to be believed, or assumes that the recipients of his statement have already made up their minds. What's the use? If it is all going to come to an end anyway . . . why should one have to bother responding to these charges? Yet Patrick submits himself to the inquiry of this earthly tribunal because he must be willing to acknowledge his sins and shortcomings as a man to his fellow men. He is not immune to the authority of his Church. He therefore offers to his peers, and to us, his manifest imperfection.

Contemplation

God created me just as I am. A perfect Being created a very imperfect product in me. I am a bundle of flaws, fears, insecurities, troubled thoughts, sinful and destructive actions, beauty, and mystery. I am the child of God. I am no better than, and no worse than, every other man and woman on the planet. My mind reels when I face the very idea of perfection that is constantly flung at me by the material world: advertising, finance, popular culture, the academy, politics, even the Church. Perfection is a chimera, a myth, a danger for me if I seek it and become a slave to it.

In fact, I do not believe in the earthly perfectibility of any one human being, especially myself, let alone all of humankind. This, despite expectations, teachings, and strivings to the contrary.

I work so hard to achieve a positive result; I usually mean well; I envision the beauty and importance of the result of my work, whether it be in my spiritual life or with my family or in my work life. But there comes a moment of paralysis, the result of perfectionism: if I cannot do it perfectly, let me not do it at all. Therefore some necessary tasks may go undone. Procrastination replaces commitment. Who suffers when this happens? I certainly do, as do others who may be dependent on me. God does not suffer, except that He is (I would imagine) disappointed in the child who chose not even to try.

I shall not dwell on the evidence of my imperfection. Neither shall I hide or cover up my imperfection. Others often see more in me than I give them credit for. And they are not as hard on me as I am on myself.

Let me really embrace this imperfect self as if he were a child who is growing into a greater knowledge and awareness of himself and contributing through his very presence, which is evidence in itself of the Father's love. I am a child of God who needs love more than anything else in the world. I need to be loved for my failings even more than for my successes.

Recently one of my sisters criticized me for being distant, unavailable to her in a time of need. She was acutely disappointed in me. I had never consciously withdrawn my affection or attention from her, yet she was correct: over a period of years I had drifted far away from her and her young family. Why? The simplest answer is acute self-centeredness. My life and my work and my family and my needs came first and occupied all of my energy and attention. I did not pick up the telephone or write a note. This may not be wrong, per se, but it is inconsiderate of others—a sin of omission. It is the opposite side of the coin to St. Patrick's imperfection: he tried so hard to reach out and bring other people to the Lord Jesus; he was selfless to the extreme, ignoring pain and danger and his own human shortcomings. He was least concerned with self.

Others will judge me—for my self-centeredness, for

my distance, for other failings—but it is possible, I believe, to learn from their judgments (just or unjust) and to gain self-awareness. I am obligated to listen to criticism for most often, I have found, there is at least a germ of truth in such negative feedback.

God speaks to us through other people. Their motives may be mixed, while His are not. But through their imperfections, as well as mine, His message comes through, if we are willing to listen for it. His love is unconditional. His care is never-ceasing. He sustained Patrick in his ministry "at the ends of the earth." How, then, can I let my own insecurities and less-then-perfect qualities block me from accomplishing anything that God wills for me?

Prayer

My prayers, my actions, my intentions, my results are imperfect in the sight of God and my fellows—yet I now pray that I may embrace my own deep and abiding imperfection, my defects and shortcomings, my very sins. For I am what You created, just as You created me, and I know that You, Father, love me, without condition or expectation, as I am. If You can love me with all my faults, why can I not love myself? You are perfect in Your being; I am not. Our Father, hear my prayer.

SACRIFICE

Could I have come here, to Ireland, without the guidance of God, or for reasons that were human and secular? Who compelled me on this mission? It is because of the Holy Spirit that I am bound to remain forever separated from my family. Does this forgiveness that I have shown to the very people who once enslaved me and pillaged the male and female servants of my father's household come from within me? In the eyes of the secular world, I am a free man, the son of a Roman decurion. But I have traded my noble birthright, without shame or second thought, for the advantage [benefit] of others. In a word, I am Christ's slave; I serve Him by ministering to foreign tribes for the sake of the indescribable glory of eternal life that is in Christ Jesus our Lord.

And if my own people will not know [appreciate] me, it is because "a prophet is without honor in his own country." Indeed, perhaps we are not of the same fold and do not have the one true

God. As He says: "He who is not with Me is against Me, and he who does not gather with Me, scatters." It is not enough [not correct] that one destroys and another builds up. I do not seek anything for myself. It was not by my own grace, but God who put within me this sincere care in my heart, that I should be one of His hunters and fishers of souls, whom God had long ago foretold would come in the end of days.

[LETTER, CH. 10–11]

Commentary

Throughout the *Confession*, but more especially in the *Letter to the Soldiers of Coroticus*, Patrick talks about the sacrifices he had to make throughout his apostleship in Ireland. He does this not in a whining or complaining way, although there is a distinct element of bitterness in his tone, but to point out that he practices what he preaches. That is, he follows the path of Christ, difficult as that undoubtedly is, to the best of his ability: this means he is willing to be separated from his own family—forever—and renounce his station in life as a Roman Briton of high birth and become a person of no status in an alien society, to rejoin those who had once kidnapped and enslaved him, to face threats and denigrations by those who oppose him in Ireland and Britain, to tread where no Christian messenger had gone before.

Coroticus was presumably of the same stock and religion as Patrick himself, "of the same fold" as the bishop puts it, whether or not his soldiers were (which is disputed among scholars of the subject). Thus Patrick was even more intensely upset at the chief's massacre of his newly baptized Christian followers. His pain is redoubled when he is compelled to censure one of his own: that is, a fellow Christian.

There is no question in his mind that the sacrifices Patrick makes are necessary; God has ordained his path, brought him to Ireland for divine purposes. Patrick claims it was not his idea in the first place, nor any man's; his reasons are not "human and secular." In fact, the Holy Spirit revealed to the saint, through dreams and visions, what he must do and where he must go. From his earliest days of faith, as a slave and shepherd on the cold but beautiful hillside, he prayed to God and listened intently for His reply. The first divine message we read about was the one Patrick received when it was time to escape captivity.

Later, in the *Confession*, we will read of other visitations and revelations that guided him through his life and ministry. He writes that he willingly became a slave of Christ, and as such he accepted a life of toil and difficulty with a glad heart. He literally sacrificed everything he had and everything he was to this cause in which he believed. In return, he was given a special role in the history of the Church in the late ancient world.

In St. Patrick's context, sacrifice inevitably means suffering. No doubt, he suffered physically and mentally from beatings and cold and starvation as a slave, from loneliness and danger and more starvation during his escape, from mockery and humiliation and isolation as a young adult seeking to catch up to others in book learning; he suffered the pangs of a guilty conscience until he revealed to a close friend, on the eve of his ordination as deacon, the terrible (he thought) sin of his youth; and in Ireland, a strange and wild land, he faced the dangers of an unknown land with hostile leaders and skeptical people, lack of support from his home diocese, fear and discontent among his staff, temptations and disappointments at every turn. Patrick was thus no stranger to suffering of many kinds, but he knew it was a fact of life in his chosen field of endeavor.

Like many passages in the writings of St. Patrick, the quotation above contains some puzzling assertions. In a sense, these paragraphs foreshadow the *Confession*, which most historians assert came later, closer to the end of his life. That document was a response to charges and criticisms Patrick had to face later in his career. But at this stage, Patrick's work is blossoming and his mission is succeeding, possibly beyond his wildest expectations. Therefore, why the defensive tone of the sentences in an epistle of excommunication? One answer lies in an appreciation of the enormity, in his mind, of what is at stake here: the fulfillment or failure of the mission of Christ.

It is quite possible that Patrick wrote with a goal beyond the immediate crisis—that he was addressing not only Coroticus and his soldiers but his colleagues in Britain and on the continent of Europe with his castigating words. Any challenge to his episcopate was a direct challenge to European (i.e., Roman) Christianity itself. In this document, Patrick begins to see the full implication of success of his mission—a lesson that will be elaborated in the *Confession*. The intensity with which he had succeeded in bringing the gospel to "the ends of the earth" convinces him of the ultimate unity of the Body of Christ throughout the Roman world, and of the ultimate unity of all humankind in the fellowship of faith.

St. Patrick's willingness to sacrifice himself, all of himself, yielded bountiful spiritual results.

Contemplation

What am I willing to sacrifice to follow God's will for me? What do I want that is worth the short-term pain for long-term gain? Do I love my family and friends enough to put myself and my own interests aside and be available to them? What does Patrick's saintly example teach me about my own values and my spiritual commitment?

It is helpful to look at sacrifice as a counterbalance to selfishness. I can very easily get wrapped up in myself, in my needs and desires. My appetites often dictate my actions. This is natural and human, and it results from basic survival instincts. But in a world of ubiquitous channels of entertainment and information, of readily available drugs and self-gratification and escape of every kind, it becomes more difficult to say no than to jump on the bandwagon of appetite fulfillment.

The Lenten season of preparation for Easter, in the Christian tradition, is an opportunity to focus on sacrifice: forty days that commemorate Christ's time of purification in the desert. During that time he was tempted repeatedly by Satan, and resisted the temptations of food, power, and pomp. Not only did Jesus cast away temptation, but he sought the help of God and was rewarded with the presence of angels to save him. Patrick, too, wrote about temptation. He says he also faced the devil directly and wrestled with evil; he ultimately made the correct choices, though it is probable that he stumbled many times along the way.

How trivial it is, then, for me to give up my nightly snack of Oreos and milk during the forty-day season of Lent. As a child, I remember the ultimate sacrifice: no TV for Lent! That was tough. Now it behooves me to seek opportunities to put aside things that turn my attention from God or my family and immediate community. The time spent in mindless escape by watching late-night television rather than reading or helping my children with their homework can be turned around into profitable time spent in useful activity.

What role does sacrifice play in my life? I can look at the financial aspect of sacrifice: My Church teaches the value of stewardship. My family circumstances are such that regular savings are important to insure some financial security or the availability of funds for that "rainy day," and when I have the resources in hand I ought to consider worthy organizations that rely upon charitable giving. It is not difficult to identify opportunities.

On the other hand, I do not need to punish myself or seek out pain. I simply need to put myself in the stream of spiritual activity that requires me to give of myself; like Patrick, I should be attuned to the call, available to help, willing to pitch in, knowledgeable enough to carry the gospel message to others in any number of simple, practical ways; following the example of Christ, I should look to God and stand with my brother.

Sacrifice is a private act, not to be shouted about. The value of a sacrificial act is private and personal, between God and the actor. The satisfaction of a job well done at some personal cost is reward enough. Dignity and communication with God result from my willingness to make sacrifices.

Prayer

Heavenly Father, grant to me that willingness to put aside thought of comfort and self-satisfaction when I am called upon to perform some task or help some person. I pray that I may seek the opportunity to make sacrifices in the service of others and to be grateful for such opportunities when they come my way. I pray that I may know that God gives me the strength, through His grace, to demonstrate my love for others through my actions.

REVELATION

ecause there is no other God, nor has there ever been, nor will there ever be, other than God the unbegotten Father, who is without beginning, from whom all has beginning, the Ruler of the universe, as we have been instructed; and His only Son Jesus Christ, whom we proclaim has always been together with the Father, and who was begotten spiritually by the Father in a way impossible to explain, before the beginning of the world, before all beginning; and by Him all things are made, visible and invisible.

Jesus was made man, and having triumphed over death was received into heaven by the Father; and the Father has given Him full power over all names in the heavens and on earth, and in hell, and every tongue shall confess to Him that Jesus Christ is Lord and God, in whom we believe, and whose second advent we expect very soon, judge of the living and of the dead who will return to every man according to what he has done. And He [God the Father] has poured out upon us so abundantly the Holy

Spirit, the gift and pledge of immortality, who makes those who believe and obey become sons of God and equal inheritors with Christ. We confess and adore Him—one God in the Trinity of the Most Holy Name.

For He has Himself said through His prophet: "Call upon Me in the day of your trial and trouble, and I will rescue you; and you shall glorify Me." And He has said: "It is honorable to reveal and preach the works of God."

[CONFESSION, CH. 4–5]

Commentary

Patrick is very closely identified with the Trinity. Just as he is traditionally depicted in religious illustrations stamping on a snake with a well-pedicured foot, he frequently holds up a shamrock to represent his teaching (to the simple-minded pagans) the doctrine of the Trinity: the "threeness in Oneness" of God's person in the Roman Catholic faith. Modern scholars seriously doubt that St. Patrick used the shamrock, the beautiful little trifoliate plant so abundant in the land of his mission, in this way. Nonetheless, there is no question as to Patrick's committed belief in the Holy Trinity. He believed in it, and he preached it to the Irish people.

Early in the *Confession* (chapter 4) he presents the Rule of Faith of the ancient Church in Britain; later (in chapter 14) he calls it the "rule of faith in the Holy Trinity." These are not his own words. He is recording in this passage a formulation of beliefs—a creed—that appears in another document. We suppose that he includes the Rule partly as a declaration of his orthodoxy, "partly to prove his credentials, but also because of its pivotal importance in his life."

[Whiteside, p. 21] The second half of his Rule (in chapter 4, above) is composed of a series of five direct quotations from New Testament sources: Paul's epistles to the Philippians, to the Romans, and to Titus, and the Acts of the Apostles. Here, as elsewhere in the *Confession*, the author quotes extensively from the Bible to bolster both his argument and his prose. Patrick clearly saw himself in the mold of Paul and the other apostles of Christ.

The Rule itself was likely promulgated in the wake of—or in response to—the great Arian heresy of the fourth century. However, the Church of Britain seems to have maintained its orthodoxy throughout the fifth century. And as Patrick's native church, it was the bedrock of his faith and his mission.

Perhaps Patrick learned the Rule as he studied for ordination. Leaving apart the question of where he received his ecclesiastical formation for holy orders—whether in Britain, Gaul, or Rome—it is interesting to note that Patrick absorbed the tenets of faith more deeply and readily than the basic skills of rhetoric. He believes what he says and cares more about content than style.

So what did he believe about the Trinity? God created the world and mankind; He sent His only Son to redeem the world from sin; He dispatched the Holy Spirit to bring light and life to the world. God so loved the world, having made it in the first place, that he must save and sanctify it—us—with His unconditional, unceasing love.

Patrick writes, "I must teach our rule of faith in the Trinity" without fear of danger to his own life. Perhaps by the time he has come to write the *Confession* his tremendous success has made him a candidate for martyrdom. Whatever the risk, he will continue to proclaim and reveal the holy name of God and baptize the converted, as he has already by the thousands.

Here is the core of St. Patrick's spirituality: a simple faith in the deepest mystery of the early Church. That faith then empowered him to do whatever God willed him to do. Of course, Patrick had a choice—many choices: to believe or not to believe, to act or to remain idle, to persevere or to give up in the face of obstacles. He found in the Trinity the complexity, the strength, the mystery of his God. How profound a step it was to accept the mystery, to embrace it, to preach it, to reveal it.

Contemplation

I do not possess the simple, unvarnished faith that St. Patrick had in the Trinity. Yet the creed I recite during the liturgy of the mass spells out clearly the same system of belief, which is reflected in Patrick's writing.

To me, the teaching of the Trinity as presented in St. Patrick's writings represents the mystery and the majesty of a Supreme Being that I cannot hope to understand in my finite state of existence. Nor is it necessary for me to do so in order to live a full spiritual life. I choose, instead, to marvel at the beauty and complexity of this ancient theological construct; I see it as an expression of the early Christians' need for a God who is real and accessible and dynamic.

The Father is, for me, the source of all existence. He breathed life into me and into all living things. He resides in me and I in His universe. I need a loving Father in my life, someone to turn to for guidance, for comfort, for purpose, for forgiveness. He is the standard to which I aspire as a human father, to which Patrick aspired as a pastor: to lead and teach our children by example. In this aspiration I fail every day. Yet God the Father does not fail—ever.

The Son, coeval and coequal to the Father, nonetheless gives us some hope in our humanity. While I say again that I do not believe in the perfectibility of man on earth, the Son taught me that it is right to strive for perfect spiritual ideals: faith, hope, love, humility, tolerance, and more. As recorded in Scriptures, His life was an act of sacrifice and example of selflessness that has never yet been matched by any other human being. I fall short of the Son's loving abnegation of self; His was a life process of "letting go" and "letting God"—unto torture and death. Would that I had the spiritual stamina and supreme trust in Him to let God rule my life. Would that I might adopt the Son's attitude of fearlessness and utter acceptance of God's will for me. For beyond death the all-forgiving, all-loving Father awaits me, His son, with open arms.

The Holy Spirit is the quiet yet powerful manifestation of God's presence in my being. The familiar symbol of the dove—snow white, pure, borne on wings of truth, touching the disciples of Christ—reassures the believer of today of the continuity of the tradition of the Holy Trinity. From the Father and the Son, according to the creed that is spoken in the liturgy of the mass, the Holy Spirit "proceeds" to move our minds and souls, to inspire our actions and words, to sustain our faith in times of difficulty. With the Father and the Son, in that same creed, the Spirit is "worshiped and glorified; He has spoken through the prophets." I believe the Holy Spirit accomplishes God's daily work on earth.

Together, the three persons are One God—and always have been, and shall be forever. This formulation of the nature of divinity, as taught in the Roman Catholic tradition, gives us an abiding and wonderful mystery to carry in our hearts as we contemplate God.

The Holy Trinity inspires some of the most beautiful language in the Patrician canon, which in itself is marvelously evocative and inspirational:

> I arise today
> > in God's mighty strength,
> > speaking in my mouth the Trinity,
> > believing in mind Three Persons,
> > confessing in heart they are One,
> > thanking my Creator.

[TRANSLATION BY G.T.]

How is this glorious enigma, wrapped in the shrouds of centuries of teaching and debate, relevant to my spiritual well-being? Isn't it an outmoded, chimerical construct, perhaps even a daydream, that differs from the moral here-and-now? On the contrary: I find it extremely helpful, when I am trying to focus on God in prayer or contemplation, to employ the images and attributes of Father, Son, and Spirit. I then have a foundation—coherent and tangible to me—upon which to worship, meditate, and supplicate.

I need all the help I can get to maintain my relationship with God; He is always willing and ever available, but I stumble and stray and forget sometimes. He will never fail me, but I fall short every single day. He is more than a Father, a Son, and a Holy Spirit—yet He is each and all of these to me.

Prayer

Hear me, Blessed Trinity, my God who is Three-in-One: God the Father, the Son, and the Holy Spirit, come into my heart. Help me to overcome my lack of belief. How beautiful it is to contemplate the glory of Patrick's teaching—the eternal existence of the Father, the sacrifice of the Son, the inspiration of the Holy Spirit. I believe that God is without beginning and without end, and that He lives within me.

GRACE

onsequently, by the light of our rule of faith in the Holy Trinity, I must make this decision, disregarding any personal danger; I must make known the gifts of God and His everlasting solace. Boldly and without any fear I must faithfully preach everywhere the name of God, so that even after my own death I might leave a spiritual legacy to my brethren and my children whom I have baptized in the Lord—so many thousands of people.

And I was in no way worthy, nor was I the sort of person that the Lord would grant such a gift to me, His humblest servant: that after my many hardships and misfortunes, after such great difficulties and burdens, after my captivity and enslavement, after so many years living among the Irish, He should give me so great a grace in behalf of this nation of people—something that once, in my boyhood, I never dreamed nor could even hope for.

[CONFESSION, CH. 14–15]

Commentary

God's grace is manifest throughout the wonderful adventure story that is Patrick's life and ministry. He speaks out "boldly" of God's gifts to him. Without God to sustain him, Patrick is nothing. No human being has the power, in and of himself, to perform such deeds as he did, nor would Patrick claim such power. He continually credited God with creating, leading, sustaining, punishing, and rewarding him—all of which is preparatory to the Lord's final judgment. God is the great Parent of all men and women. We are called to obey Him as a child must obey a Father; in turn, God does not withhold His love and healing from us, nor does He base His dispensation of these gifts on our personal worthiness to receive them.

By our very nature, our simple existence, we have received God's greatest gift. Grace, then, represents the further gifts and blessings and, indeed, miracles that occur in our lives. To paraphrase theologian Paul Tillich, it is at our darkest and emptiest moments that we are stricken, or blessed, by grace.

This quite accurately describes Patrick's experience: as a captive of a barbarian (i.e., non-Roman) race, held far from his home in Britain, he was as cut off from his origins as he could be, and there was little to no hope of escape from enslavement. It does not get much darker or emptier than that. Yet, Patrick was touched by the presence of God and prompted to pray, to reach out for help from that seemingly distant Supreme Power.

Grace, in another way of putting it, is God's supply of strength: Patrick claimed and proclaimed God's strength. He needed every ounce of physical and mental strength to carry the gospel to the so-called heathens of this distant island. The druidic religion was deeply embedded in the land, and his task was to offer an alternative—what he believed to be the true faith—before it was too late for the Irish people. For Patrick the missionary bishop, the dispensation of grace resided in the sacraments of the Church. First, he must baptize those who converted after he had evangelized them; then, these souls newly found for Christ must be confirmed in their faith. The Eucharist and penance bound these souls closer to the Body of Christ. Priestly ordination brought men into the Lord's service, and marriage—Christian marriage—brought women and men together in God's sight. Finally, the last rites at death ushered the Christian soul to God, whole and forgiven of sins.

Patrick never tired of preaching the gospel and practicing the sacraments. By the thousands, he tells us, he brought the people to Christ. He writes about this heroic effort somewhat defensively—rather than boastfully—for he is, after all, defending himself in the *Confession* and enumerating his accomplishments. Yet always he gives credit to God, who, by gracing Patrick's mission, has wrought these events.

The legendary life of St. Patrick is an embellishment upon the theme of God's grace. The bishop is a miracle worker par excellence in the later *Lives*, overthrowing idols, besting druid priest-magicians at their own game, calling upon the vast powers of the Almighty to settle petty quarrels and wreak vengeance upon unbelievers. But in the true life—so much as we are able to understand and reconstruct it—lies the wonder of true miracles. Although he does not claim any of the myriad miracles that are attributed to him in legend, Patrick does relate, especially in the *Confession*, how God communicated with him directly through dreams and visions. He also rather astutely anticipates critics and unbelievers: "Let anyone who wishes to laugh and mock me do so, for I will not be silent, nor will I refrain from revealing the signs and wonders that the Lord has shown to me many years before they came to pass, for He knows all that is to occur since before the very beginning of time." [*Confession*, ch. 45]

Miracles, the direct result of God's grace, in good times and bad, seemed to follow Patrick wherever he went. These were not only the visions, but the change he accomplished on a grand scale, the conversion of virtually an entire nation, to Christian belief. Yet, with Christ as his example, Patrick claimed no special powers as his own; through the Father's grace alone did he have such a successful ministry.

Patrick writes specifically about leaving a spiritual legacy to "my brethren and my children." He did, and that legacy is a witness to the grace of God. For how else did he—do any of us—achieve spiritual growth and material security but through that grace? The key for Patrick was his openness to receive the grace that God so urgently wanted to give.

Contemplation

In my life, God's grace works with amazing effectiveness, despite my sometimes deep unworthiness to receive it, despite my resistance or lack of faith. God gives me these gifts freely, despite myself.

I believe that God is ever willing and ready to distribute His blessings to me in the most generous measure conceivable. However, like the sowing of the seed illustrated in the Gospel, the ground—the soul—must be prepared before the seed is scattered upon it. It is my task, therefore, to prepare the soil. It is God's job—and His right—to distribute the seed. In order to prepare myself to receive the seed, the gift, I cultivate the soil, the soul, by trying my best to live properly, to choose the right path and avoid the wrong way.

Each day, I can cultivate and prepare myself for the sowing of the seed of His love in the form of His blessings. Before I know it, the harvest time will come. Then I confront another series of choices as to how to share the abundant harvest with my fellows and my gratitude with God. He is the Source of my useful and more abundant life.

"Grace is the love and generosity of God which comes through no effort of our own." [*Touchstones: A Book of Daily Meditations for Men,* Sept. 18] But often, it is not until I feel defeated in some ambition or made low by my own actions that I turn to my Creator for help; I forget, in the course of daily activities, where all good things come from in the first place.

Grace comes when I need it, but not necessarily when I ask for it. Also, it comes in many different forms: it is in a quiet morning walk with my partner; it is in the shy smile of my child; it is in the moment of consecration at mass; it is in the good feeling after a phone call to a friend; it is in a good night's sleep. These are simple, pleasurable examples of grace. But I must be aware of my surroundings, divorced from my self-centeredness, to receive the healing message in each manifestation of God's grace.

In God I find consolation and comfort. I seek relief from the difficulties of my life in this troubled world. I seek answers to questions that disturb me. I seek to be liberated from the prison of my own thoughts and prejudices. Sometimes, when I am trying to control my life and dictate the results of others' actions, I am separated from God and His grace. At these times I am moving farther from God. It is necessary, then, for me to reverse course and begin moving *toward* God. I think this is all he asks of me: to try my best to be with Him, to be attuned to His will. Grace, then, is His measured effort to bring me close and keep me close.

The grace of God can remedy disharmony between people. I have experienced this directly: when I have prayed for those with whom I have been in conflict (whether through dislike, disagreement, or different goals), I have found that the source of that conflict or the intensity of the conflict has been dissolved. I must be willing, however, to do something that is difficult for me: to pray for someone whom I fear or do not like. Yet, when I consider it, I realize that this is a very private activity, a one-on-one with my Supreme Being, that I can do at any time, any place. Like so much in the spiritual life, it requires only that I take a simple, quiet step, and trust that God will supply the rest in the form of His grace.

As in the Prayer of St. Francis, I am the channel or the vessel into which God's grace flows—if I keep that channel open, if I empty the vessel of my own thoughts, fears, and expectations, my pride, selfishness, and defensiveness.

The evidence of God's grace in my life, therefore, is abundant, if I am awakened to it through prayer, worship, and study. Am I ready to receive these blessings in my life? Do I pass along His grace to others?

God's greatest grace is His very presence. He graced Patrick with incredible strength and understanding of his purpose, and He graces us each day in tangible ways that we can know, if we are looking for them.

Prayer

When I fall, Heavenly Father, You pick me up. When I fail to believe, You grant me Your unconditional love. When I am in pain, You heal me. When I am in darkness, You light the way. These are Your graces that You grant me even in my unworthiness. These are not rewards or accomplishments, but free gifts that I am free to accept or reject. You surround me with love and gifts. I pray that I may accept Your grace and share Your grace with others.

ANGER

J am the target of resentment and jealousy. What shall I do, O Lord? I am openly despised. Look, all around me Your sheep lie torn and spoiled, and by these very soldiers of Coroticus at his evil orders. Far removed from the love of God is anyone who betrays my newly won Christian into the hands of the Scots and Picts. Voracious wolves have eaten the Lord's flock, just when it was increasing in Ireland with tender care. How many sons of Scots kings and daughters of Pictic chiefs have become monks and virgins of Christ—I cannot count their number. So do not be pleased by this calamity; it is unacceptable, unjust, and irredeemable all the way to hell.

So who among the holy saints would not shudder to make merry or partake of a feast with men such as these? They have filled their houses with the stolen property of dead Christians; they live only to plunder. These wretched men do not know that it is poison that they offer as food to their children and their friends, just as Eve did not realize that it was certain death she *was offering to her husband. But so it is always with those who commit such evil: their earthly work brings only the eternal punishment of death.*

However, the custom of the Christian Romans of Gaul is different: they send holy and capable men to the Franks and other heathen nations with as many thousands of solidi as required to ransom baptized captives. But you [Coroticus] murder them or sell them to a foreign race who do not know of our true God; you might as well hand over the members of Christ to a brothel. What hope could you then have in the grace of God, or could anyone have who agrees with you, or who speaks with you, or who shows you any measure of respect? God Himself will surely judge. For it is written, "not only those who do evil, but those who consent to it will be condemned."

[LETTER, CH. 12–14]

Commentary

Like the prophets of the Hebrew Bible, St. Patrick was angry when he was confronted with depredations within his missionary diocese. He could not have been surprised, really, but he was taken aback by the viciousness of the men under the command of Coroticus. He was righteous in his anger, even as he acknowledges his own unworthiness and position as one disrespected openly and widely. Patrick knows he is on a slippery slope here, but he cannot contain his anger.

Further, he seeks to foment anger among his fellow Christians, and advises them that they must not sit with evildoers: "So who among the holy saints would not shudder to make merry or partake of a feast with men such as these?" He warns that the result of the actions of these "wretched" men, Coroticus and his army, will be eternal punishment for them, as it is for all sinners who commit such grievous crimes.

Another cause of Patrick's deeper anger is the violation of accepted practices even in the unnatural state of war. Why do the soldiers of the warlord not ransom their captives as is done on the European continent? What they have done in this case is beyond the pale even in a society well used to warfare and slavery. To Patrick, this attack not only counts as victims the poor souls killed and taken hostage, but also endangers the apostle's entire mission of spreading Christianity to the farthest ends of the known world. St. Patrick seems to think that these newly baptized Christians might be seen by the soldiers as less than worthy of inclusion in the Christian community. After all, he himself is despised for his actions; what business does he, a free-born Roman Briton, have proselytizing among the Irish? But he reminds the reader of the letter that Christians all over Europe are ransoming Christian captives and rescuing them from sale into slavery under heathens.

The bishop addresses the Romanized Britons, his own people, with respect by comparing them to the Roman Gauls. Both considered themselves high-born classes within the empire, yet the latter will spare no expense (paying in the gold currency, with the *solidi*, a gold coin first struck by Constantine) to redeem captured Christians. So, he has shifted the focus of the argument, briefly, from a straightforward rebuke of the marauding soldiers to an appeal to Christians far and wide to regard the fate of these newly baptized captives as of importance to them, to their interests as members of the Christian community.

The struggle is a universal one—it goes all the way back to Adam and Eve, and to their sons Cain and Abel, in

Genesis—and it transcends national boundaries. There is no task of greater urgency, in Patrick's mind. His audience must feel his emotion and his authority.

Although God Himself will eventually judge the sinners, Patrick, as God's servant and representative on earth, has the authority and the obligation to call them to account here and now.

Contemplation

Anger is a necessary and inevitable emotion. Anger differentiates me and creates borders between me and the behavior of other people. When my spouse or a family member does not listen to me, I become angry. When a coworker lets me down or undermines me, I get angry. When a public figure says something stupid or hurtful that I read about in the newspaper, I am disturbed. There are innumerable other cases, large and small, that I could cite—just for a single day.

In normal activities it is expected that we will encounter other people; this makes conflict between human beings unavoidable. So what can I do about anger?

Well, first I must be wary of self-righteous or justified anger. There *are* times when I am right and the other person is wrong; there *are* behaviors that are offensive or hurtful to me; there *are* situations when I feel I must defend another (a friend, a child, a colleague) against actions that might be harmful to him. Yet, the tendency to wrap oneself in the mantle of righteousness is often wrong in itself and can be self-destructive. It can blind one to consequences, fuel inappropriate reactions. For this reason, I am on guard against giving in completely to justified anger. It is important that I stop and think—say a prayer, perhaps, or take a walk—before I speak or act in anger, even if I am 100 percent right.

I wonder what St. Patrick was feeling as he wrote of the crimes of these men against fellow Christians. It is clear in his sharp words that he was deeply affected by their fate. And even in the context of a dangerous world of constant conflict, the behavior of the Christian soldiers violated the norms of warfare and its aftermath. It is also clear from the harsh tone of the *Letter* that Patrick was writing it while the offenses were very recent. They required an immediate response—and so, his anger was fresh and red-hot.

I can identify with his position, and I think all of us can: while we rarely encounter so directly the effects of evil, we are inundated with reports in various media, day after day, of heinous crimes and assaults by people against people. Wars and pogroms and genocides are chronicled in the daily press—not just in the history books. In such time anger—deep, true anger—is justified and moral. I can understand how a pastor would shed tears and denounce anyone who so destroyed his flock. I can feel, palpably in Patrick's words, the rage of the man.

However, I must remember that when I am on the side of right and angry at the wrongdoer, I am skirting an occasion of sin myself. After all, anger is one of the seven deadly sins. I believe this is so because it flows from and may cause other sins. Anger is as fluid and as difficult to contain as mercury. It may come suddenly or build up slowly; it may crash like a tidal wave or settle like a mist over the landscape.

If I honestly examine the role of anger in my life, I can identify patterns and phases, particular touchstones, that demonstrate how I handle anger—or, perhaps more accurately, how it handles me. Anger—righteous, petty, passing, or debilitating—is a real fact of life.

At the same time, while recognizing its destructive aspects, I must accept anger for what it is and not bottle it up and deny it. I did not learn this important lesson as a child. I did not learn this as a young adult trying to make my way in the world. But I have, finally in midlife, learned to accept but not succumb to anger. I have learned how to express my anger constructively, not destructively. I have learned, with the help of my family, that anger erupts with those you love most and—very importantly—that I do not have to let an angry moment ruin my entire day.

Prayer

O God, I offer to you my anger at other people, a heavy and painful emotion that is difficult for me to handle on my own. You can handle it better than I can. Help me, when I become angry, to pause and seek your presence, to pray and think through the situation, to remember that the object of my anger is a person of worth with problems and virtues. I wish not to be an angry person, but one filled with love and gratitude. Hear my prayer.

INDIVIDUAL
WORTH

*A*nd there was a special, blessed woman of Irish origin—noble in rank, mature and beautiful—whom I had baptized. She came to us a few days later and told us in private that she had received a message from an angel of God who inspired her to become a virgin of Christ and to draw nearer to Him. Thanks be to God for just six days afterward, she embraced eagerly and sincerely those vows that all the virgins of God follow. They do not have their fathers' consent; rather, they often endure all manner of persecution and false accusations from their own parents. Nevertheless their number increases ever more until we cannot know how many of our race have been thus reborn, as well as the number of widows and women who live a life of chastity.

But the women who are held in slavery—they are the ones who suffer most. They must endure constant threats and terror every day. But the Lord has bestowed His grace on many of *these, His handmaids, for although they are forbidden [by their elders], they courageously follow the example of their sisters.*

So that, even if I wished to leave them and journey to Britain—and I was, with all my heart, ready and anxious to return to my homeland and my parents, and even more, to continue on to Gaul and visit the brethren and be in the presence of the saints of my Lord (how I desired it!)—I am bound by the Spirit, who has testified to me that I should be judged guilty if I were to do this. And I am fearful of destroying the work that I have begun [were I to leave]—and it is not just me, for the Lord Christ commanded me to come and live among them for the rest of my life. I pray it is the Lord's will to protect me from every evil, so that I may not sin in His sight.

[*Confession*, ch. 42–43]

Commentary

Here Patrick tells us much about individual worth and his mission to the Irish. We already know that Patrick was not the first cleric to attempt bringing Christianity to Ireland; the first, Palladius, met a quick end just before Patrick's arrival, and throughout the *Confession*, one gets the sense that the church is hesitant to send *anyone* to Ireland—that the uncertainties regarding Patrick are secondary. Patrick has told us about the vision that has sent him back to Ireland on a mission to bring Christianity to that land, but we can't help but wonder what drove him, and what made him believe he would have any better chance than his predecessor.

The culture of Ireland in the centuries before the arrival of Patrick has been vividly portrayed by many; the Celtic tradition is a rich one and the allure of the druidic wisdom-religion has spurred periodic revivals right to the present day. But what is that allure? Patrick knew it well from the days of his captivity, and he certainly dealt with it in the course of his mission. The many legends and fanciful histories regarding Patrick stem from a kernel of an idea that permeates the *Confession* and everything we know about Patrick's career and its aftermath: Patrick was anything but a passive, inactive, pacifistically unmilitant adversary. He used armed might when it was necessary, force when it was justified, and he paid for both favor and protection from the local warlords of any area in which he was active or traveling through (and he will tell us later what that cost him). The legends bespeak Patrick's strength and willingness to match might with might. But the battle Patrick waged, and won, really took place within the minds of the people of Ireland.

The druids viewed the world in what we might call *miasmic* terms. The illusion we have of things being discrete, of objects and people having a material (call it an existential) integrity—that things and people stand alone and unconnected—is just that: an illusion. The fact is that everything in the world weaves into everything else and melds into existence, like the roots of a tree dig into and become enmeshed into the earth. While the Greeks were impressed with the crystalline separateness of everything and how clearly objects stood out in the Aegean sunlight, the druids saw an effluent mist of everything permeating everything else; even thoughts wove in and out of people and nature like the wispy tendrils of a rolling fog.

The wisdom developed by the druids maintained the reality of what we know to be true: everything is connected to its surroundings; things flow into things, thoughts into thought, people into the earth and back again. The system that would derive from this approach would be open and pluralistic: receptive of wisdom or insight from wherever it came. It would see the person as not quite a separate entity, but inured into an earthly ground of existence.

The druids developed this approach into a complex system of rituals, and one of them may have included human sacrifice. Now, scholars cannot say for certain if the druids actually practiced human sacrifice in the period before Patrick. It seems now that some of that went on, for human sacrifice was not all that rare anywhere in the ancient world, particularly as a means of dealing with criminals and prisoners of war. In many of the historical instances of human sacrifice, the victims went willingly, even happily, believing they were headed for some higher communion with being. This is the system with which Patrick contends, and it will be as easy to simply dismiss the pagans and their beliefs

Patrick knows that the outcome of the contest will not be determined by trivial consensus; the druids have already demonstrated their allure. The contest, the debate, if you will, will revolve around a simple dispute: They (the druids) say people do not count, people do not even exist as separate entities; Patrick replies that that is all that counts, and not just people in numbers, but each one, each and every one.

The argument Patrick adduces is simple. His answer is "a special, blessed noblewoman of Irish origin—noble in rank, mature and beautiful" and the difference her belief has made in her life. Yes, there are minions, but Patrick's victory is to be counted by what one person does when she does it.

This is how Patrick sees his own career: not as part of a "campaign" to be furthered by his family as his work would further their interests, but as the solitary mission of a man heeding a calling and embarking on a mission, with enough of what he requires and at the same time without nearly enough.

Contemplation

I feel such an affinity with Patrick because I recognize (or think I recognize) a commonality between the system he is combating and the values of the society I live in—more particularly, the "cyberculture" that is blossoming (or is the right word *mushrooming*?) before our very eyes. I see a conviviality between the values of the digital world—in which everything exists only in terms of its connectedness to everything else, and nothing other than the keystroke has any reality—and the values of the druids of Patrick's age and throughout history. Turning people into streams of information is a short step away from believing they are nothing more than that, and that's a short step away from believing no stream of information is any more worthwhile or significant than any other. Is it hysterical to believe that soon the data become what's important, what "really exists," and the rest becomes a phantasm?

Posh, you say. The rantings of a technophobe, or someone too lazy to "get with the program." Theorists have already pointed out that the digitization of the world has as a consequence the devaluing of theory itself. The elegance of a theory that provides answers from a few manageably coherent principles becomes less something to be sought. Answers are replaced with ever more refined approximations, and soon it is enough that the machine understands what is going on, even if we don't. But it's not the theorists I worry about. It's us I worry about. The old bugaboo about fearing the day when everyone becomes a number has graduated from the world of metaphor into the world of reality: in the cyberworld everyone is, really is, a number, or a data stream.

In the midst of his defense of his mission, his episcopate, his life, Patrick can speak of the noblewoman as "mature and beautiful." He can admire her vision and her courage in defying her father and entering into her vows of chastity. Patrick is not unaware of the numbers—of the fact that many such individuals have taken such vows and at the same cost. We hear in his words, however, the presence of that woman, as if she were sitting beside him as he penned those words.

Here comes the torrent of humanity: people by the millions, billions, crossing our paths in such dizzying array that we can barely keep track. At what point does the crush become too much for us to handle? It becomes easier to be in contact with people some other way. We can do it while we're walking down the street; at any given moment I can look out on Sixth Avenue and see a dozen people walking in rapt conversation on their cell phones! And, of course, they're oblivious to the people all around them; I sometimes think they could pass their most cherished loved one on the street and not notice. The means of achieving notoriety or fame so exceed those of a few years ago that Andy Warhol's fifteen minutes have deflated to a few seconds; there are just too many people to allow anybody a full quarter of an hour.

But what significance do anyone's actions have in the context of the eternity of time and the infinity of the cosmos? Any one person's achievements have always been a minuscule blip in time, only they seem now to pale into insignificance immediately. How will this change us? How will we react to this new anonymity, one that shatters even the momentary illusion of illustriousness? How ironic that at a time when fame and celebrity are sought and valued more than at any time in human history, the very factors that make that the case conspire to render that celebrity of little consequence.

More than a millennium and a half after it happened, the delight Patrick has taken in the sincere commitment of a certain Irish noblewoman, and his loving support of her—that we know and remember, and celebrate.

Prayer

Lord, I am a single solitary person, and You see me as that person, alone, standing apart, in a sea of people, of creatures, of worlds. Nothing I accomplish could endure in this sea; my worth in Your eyes must be simply as I am, what I am, who I am. I pray You see me that way. One person. Lord, let me be a person of worth in Your eyes.

HONESTY

ut what help are excuses, however true, especially if combined with the presumption [audacity] of old age? I attempt to gain something at this stage that I did not achieve in my youth. At that time my own sins prevented me from understanding in my mind what I had previously just barely read. But who believes me now, even if I should reiterate what I have already said?

As a youth—that is, as a beardless boy unable to articulate my thoughts—I was taken captive before I knew what to pursue in my life and what to avoid. So today I blush and fear more than anything to reveal my lack of education. For I lack the skill to tell my story to those versed in the art of concise writing [learned men]—in such a way that my soul and mind long to do, and so that the sense of my words expresses what I really mean.

Indeed, if advantages had been given to me as they were to others, then I would not be silent, but I would be able to express my gratitude. Perhaps some people think me arrogant for doing so, in spite of my lack of learning and my slow tongue. After all, it is written: "The stammering tongues shall quickly learn to speak peace."

How much more should we earnestly strive to do this, we who are, so Scripture says, a letter of Christ for salvation even to the utmost ends of the earth, and though not an eloquent one, yet . . . written in your hearts not with ink, but with the spirit of the living God! And again the Spirit witnesses that even rusticity [backwardness] was made by the Most High Creator. . . .

I have written enough. However, I must not hide God's gift, which he generously gave me in the country of my captivity. Because then I sincerely sought Him and there I found Him. He protected me from evil because, I fervently believe, His Spirit lives within me and works within me even to this day. Yes, I speak this truth boldly, yet God knows if the voice had been that of a man, I might have remained silent for the love of Christ.

[CONFESSION, CH. 10–11, 33]

Commentary

"Patrick dwells almost obsessively on his lack of learning," writes John Skinner in his new translation of the *Confession* and the *Letter*. "He is particularly sensitive about his lack of the verbal skills he sees in others. Yet when he speaks so poignantly of being unable to voice the innermost meaning of his soul, we recognize the tongue-tied mystic who may not utter what he knows in his heart." [Skinner, p. 33]

We have seen this demonstrated over and over again in the aging bishop's struggle to communicate his message clearly and concisely. There are passages in his works that are virtually indecipherable, perhaps partly due to poor copying of the original, but more likely because Patrick himself was unable to express himself adequately. Thus he resents "the others," *vos dominicati rethorici,* perhaps the professional scholars and churchmen of Gaul and Britain: we know them in our century as the pedants and "highbrows" who haughtily put themselves above those who are less skilled in the arts of language.

Nowhere, however, is there a word or sentence that does not ring with the authority of pure honesty. Patrick believed what the Scriptures taught him about truth and lies. First, that bearing false witness is a sin against the commandments. Second, that lies in any form are unacceptable to a just God. Third, that those who lie or cause others to lie will be judged accordingly on the last day. Therefore, it was not style that determined the value of his message, but content.

An important aspect of Patrick's basic honesty is his ability to point to himself and his sins, to be unsparingly self-critical before the world. Patrick strove to tell the whole truth in answer to a series of accusations, as if he were in the witness stand in court. He did not hold back the ugly truth, as he saw it; he laid it all out for others to judge, withholding nothing.

On the eve of his ordination as deacon—thirty years before the writing of his *Confession,* if we read him correctly— Patrick confessed to a dear friend a sin he had committed before his time of captivity. The sin itself would have occurred when he was younger than sixteen; thus it was the act of an immature person. It was important enough to him to confess, to enter the service of the Church with a clean slate.

At some later point when his accusers were building a

case against him and his mission, they were able to dredge up this old sin. His close friend became an accuser. Thus Patrick paid a high price for his honesty. Hugh De Blácam writes of the betrayal and its aftermath:

How can we explain this strange and deplorable act? We know the type of character, ardent and inconstant, that is capable of such whims. The friend of our saint spoke words that galled Patrick to his life's end.

In some intimate talk, Patrick once had told this brother in religion of a sin that he had committed in boyhood—something that he "had done one day, nay in one hour," before he was fifteen years old, and before he had grown strong in virtue or acquired the faith that came to him in his years of trial. This fault Patricius had disclosed through a scruple before he received the diaconate, ten years earlier; and now the friend to whom he had imparted the secret disclosed it to his superiors.

We may suppose that the fault was one of presumption—some youthful, ambitious boast, perhaps—for manifestly it was something that seemed incompatible with the desire for leadership of a mission. Suppose it was said: "This Patricius, who now asks your reverences to entrust him with high responsibility, boasted in youth that he would be a great man; he is proud and arrogant, on his own admission." Suspicion of a fault of this kind is just what would destroy the hopes which Patrick cherished in all humility. However that may be, the false friend's disclosure did result both in the disappointment of the would-be missionary and in his public humiliation. [De Blácam, *Saint Patrick,* pp. 33–34]

The betrayal of confidence by a friend to whom Patrick had honestly confessed a sin—whether it was bound by the sacramental or not—was a blow that rankled some thirty, or more, years later.

I sense that it was a more severe sin than De Blácam describes in his account of Patrick's time of trial. Perhaps it was an occurrence of sexual misconduct by the adolescent. Even today we can feel the intensity of Patrick's honest self-appraisal in virtually every passage of the *Confession*. It cannot have been easy for him to reveal himself with such unabashed candor, nor easy for his contemporaries—whether they liked him or not—to read such truth-telling. However, on the issue of the exact nature of his youthful crime, there simply is no evidence to prove one way or the other what the offense was. We must take Patrick's words and, I believe, his motivation at face value.

If there is a difference between overt honesty and honesty of motive —that is, if you can have one without the other—Patrick surely displays both. Although he is defensive, he is not lording his righteousness over his accusers or anyone else. He does not build himself up by tearing others down. Patrick has the courage to be completely, boldly honest, to challenge himself as well as his accusers. He trusts that they will act rightly, given the truth, as he has expressed it.

He believes that "the truth shall set you free" and this is the core of what he preached. And he practices what he preaches.

Contemplation

Honesty is simple, but it is not always easy for me. I am a complicated human being, with needs and aspirations and shortcomings. In the Judeo-Christian tradition, based on the Ten Commandments, lying, or "bearing false witness against thy neighbor," is a sin. In practical, secular terms, lying is wrong, and such behavior causes problems, hurts others, erodes one's own moral standing.

Yet honesty is more than just not lying. Patrick's example is a powerful one: scorching self-exposure was his approach. This is extremely difficult, yet it is an ideal for all of us to strive for.

"Only God can fully know what absolute honesty is. Therefore, each of us has to conceive what this great ideal may be—to the best of our ability. Fallible as we all are, and will be in this life, it would be presumption to suppose that we could ever really achieve absolute honesty. The best we can do is to strive for a better quality of honesty." [Bill W., *As Bill Sees It,* p. 172] Do I trust God to guide me, to give me the strength to be honest with myself and others?

Honesty, in fact, may be seen as an antidote to fear. What a great relief it is to tell the truth—even an unpleasant or difficult truth—rather than to fabricate a story or cover up the reality of a situation. I have been guilty of fudging the truth in uncomfortable situations, and I have paid the price for this action. Inevitably, the truth will come back to haunt me, and I will be forced to face it, to admit it, to repair the damage done.

Honesty is also a path to true friendship. Despite Patrick's experience of betrayal, I have found that it is healthy and necessary to be scrupulously truthful with friends. A relationship based on honesty is not hurt-free. With those closest to me, I feel comfortable sharing the darker side of myself and listening to their constructive criticism. Both are shared with love. To withhold truth is to withhold feeling. Friends trust each other with the truth.

This experience of total trust, with friends, with my spouse, with my spiritual director, with God, allows me to face myself more frankly, to hold myself accountable for my actions—thus I achieve self-knowledge, the fruit of honesty. Did Patrick have any close friends in his ministry? Did he have a spouse (marriage of priests was not proscribed at that time; his father and grandfather had married and fathered sons) or close companion in those years? His primary relationship was, clearly, with God; through prayer and Bible study and evangelizing, Patrick kept himself always close to God. And he accepted responsibility for his sins and character flaws.

When I drop my defenses and expose myself to consequences, as Patrick did, I become vulnerable. I must rid myself of little secrets and skeletons in the closet, of the self-deceptions that drag me down. I must make myself vulnerable in this way, in personal relationships and other aspects of my life; I must trust God to keep me safe, to pick me up when I stumble, to put good people in my life, to give me the ability to like myself and to love myself even when I am guilty of doing something wrong or not being completely truthful. My God will give me the ability to correct my mistakes, as long as I acknowledge them and strive to do better next time.

If I try today to act with complete honesty of motive, to speak the truth to others, to be completely honest with myself, I will achieve incredible spiritual results. How freeing it is to put away my long-held defenses when others are honest with me! Do I tell the truth always? Do I truly listen when others speak honestly to me?

Prayer

I pray that my life may be founded on the bedrock of honesty: honesty with self, with others, with God. I ask for the courage to be honest in every aspect of my life. Please, Father, remove any block to the light of Your truth, Your will for me today. I believe that the truth shall set me free to be the best person possible. Grant me the strength to examine my motives and actions that they may be in accord with Your will. I seek Your help with the knowledge of my faults and failings, for I cannot overcome them alone.

PRAYER

ut after I was taken to Ireland [as a slave]—then every day I was forced to tend flocks of sheep in the pasture. As I did so, many, many times throughout the day I prayed. The love of God and the awe [fear] of Him grew strong within me more and more, and my faith was strengthened also. And my soul was restless within me so that in a single day I would say as many as a hundred prayers, and almost as many in the night, and this even when I was staying in the woods or on the mountainside. I often awakened and prayed before daylight—through snow, through frost, through rain— and I felt no illness or discomfort, and I was never lazy but filled with energy and inspiration. Now I know this was because the Holy Spirit was fervent [glowing] within me. . . .

Once again [on another night] I saw Him praying within me, and it was as if He were in my body. And I heard Him over me, that is, over my inner self, and He was praying mightily and groaning. All the while I was astonished and amazed, wondering *who it could be who was praying within me. But at the end of the prayer, He spoke to me, saying that He was the Spirit. At that I awoke, and I remembered what the apostle had said: "The Spirit helps the weaknesses of our prayers. For we know not what we should pray for or how. But the Spirit Himself intercedes for us with indescribable groanings that cannot be expressed in words." And it is also written: "The Lord Himself is our advocate and asks on our behalf."*

[CONFESSION, CH. 16, 25]

Commentary

No single activity was more important to St. Patrick than prayer: direct, constant communication with his God. He also sought the mediation of Christ, the Holy Spirit, the Blessed Mother, and the saints. He learned about prayer from St. Paul's epistles, and the example of Christ in the Gospels.

As we have seen, his youth was not infused with spirituality. Patrick, or Sucatus as he was then known, did not heed the teachings of the Church. He was a young Roman Briton with matters other than God on his mind:

The young Patrick, by his own admission, was far from a saint. His references to himself throughout his Confession as a sinner are in the mood and style of apostolic and religious writing of his day and times, but he admits that he turned from God as a youth, that he did not keep His commandments or obey the priests, and not only Christian but secular teaching went in one ear and out the other. He must have been a scandal to his grandfather, old Potitus the priest, who no doubt lectured

> him and prophesied a bad end for him unless he
> mended his ways. The younger generation in Bannaven
> Taburniae [sic?], it seems, was exactly what it is in every
> age and in every land. [Gallico, p. 22]

Thus it is frankly miraculous that in the solitude of the wilderness, cut off from family and familiar surroundings, Patrick found God—or God found him. The boy turned to prayer as his only means of solace, to keep his young mind focused on his salvation.

In chapter 16 of the *Confession*, Patrick describes very movingly the physical situation of his captivity: isolation from other human beings, snow, frost, rain, difficult terrain, day and night. His youthful energy did not flag, but he grew stronger through prayer—constant, repetitious, sincere. He came to know the Holy Spirit, to become infused with the spirit. Here, we may say, was the conversion or awakening of the future saint.

In the *Confession* there are a few other direct references to prayer. During his escape from slavery, after he had first been refused passage on the ship, Patrick stopped to pray. "And before I had even ended my prayer," [ch. 18] he was recalled and invited aboard. His need was answered and a human judgment reversed, before he could even finish his prayer!

The Holy Spirit visited Patrick when he had returned home to Britain [ch. 25]: "And again I saw Him praying within me, and it was as if He were in my body. And I heard Him over me, that is, over my inner self."

The Holy Spirit is our Guide in prayer, supporting and directing us. At one point Patrick quotes St. Paul and the Gospel of John: "The Spirit helps the weaknesses of our prayers. For we know not what we should pray for or how. But the Spirit Himself intercedes for us with indescribable groanings that cannot be expressed in words. . . . The Lord Himself is our advocate and asks on our behalf." [ch. 25]

Much later in his life, Patrick the bishop, as he faced old age, as he answered accusations from fellow clerics in Britain, as he looked back on his accomplishments and failures, stripped away all but the most essential content of his prayer. "I pray that God will grant his humble son perseverance and will allow me to give faithful testimony of Him until the time of my own passing, all for the sake of my God." [ch. 58] In other words, let me live long enough and grant me enough strength to tell the people of Your love—until the day I die! This sums up Patrick's mission as he saw it.

Prayer defined his relationship with God and formed the basis of every deed and decision of his life. We can draw a parallel with the prayer life of Pope John Paul II, who is reported to pray several hours a day, wherever he might be and whatever the state of his health. He often prostrates himself upon the floor, "closets" himself as Jesus taught, and focuses his entire being on prayer. This image of a twentieth-century pontiff is startlingly similar to the image we see of a fifth-century man whose entire body is possessed by the Spirit in prayer.

> Besides his [Patrick's] daily care of the churches, his invincible spirit never slackened in prayer. For it is said that he was wont to recite every day the whole Psalter, together with the Canticles and Hymns, and two hundred prayers; that he every day knelt down three hundred times to adore God; and that at each canonical hour of the day, he signed himself a hundred times with

the sign of the cross. He divided the night into three parts; first, he repeated the first hundred Psalms, and genuflected two hundred times; the second was spent in reciting the remaining fifty Psalms, standing in cold water, with his heart, eyes, and hands lifted up to heaven; the third he gave to a little sleep, stretched upon a bare stone. Remarkable for his practice of humility, like the Apostles, he did not abstain from manual labor.

—From the Office for the Feast of St. Patrick,
Bishop and Confessor, March 17

It is one of the most compelling spiritual images in the history of Christian literature: a young slave, a sheepherder in foreign captivity, standing in the snow or rain on a rugged mountainside, friendless (possibly), torn from the bosom of his family, as we know from his own testimony. He is praying intensely, perhaps repetitiously, to a God he had turned to out of desperation. We may picture him with his arms upraised, hands open to grasp any tangible form of God's grace.

And there was no ending to his prayers. Morning, noontime, and night he prayed. Patrick, by his accounting, prayed hundreds of prayers daily during his six-year captivity. We may presume that, as a free man during his years of study and preparation to be ordained, he prayed at least as much. As a missionary bishop with a world-changing task before him—carrying the gospel message to the ends of the earth—he certainly could not cease praying. In fact, it is most likely that he devoted as much time as possible each day to prayer.

The point is, Patrick turned his attention and energy to

God. Patrick acknowledged that God was, in fact, his "boss." " Even absent from the Roman order under which he was raised, he accepted a hierarchy of authority. This hierarchy was a necessary, indeed sacred, manifestation of God's will for mankind, he believed.

The world beyond the British Isles was devolving into chaos. Patrick found a fixed purpose and structure in the Church.

Contemplation

Prayer works. It is the most valuable, practical tool we have for construction of our own spiritual house.

In the Roman Catholic tradition, many of us were taught the Apostles' Creed, the Our Father (Lord's Prayer), the Hail Mary, the Gloria (Glory Be), the Act of Contrition, grace before meals, and other formulas. At mass or praying the rosary, we recited these prayers at prescribed times— ritualistically, often by rote. Penance, after the sacrament of confession, was often prescribed by the priest as a certain number of Our Fathers and a certain number of Hail Marys, "after a good Act of Contrition." These prayers became a familiar part of the fabric of our spiritual lives and laid the foundation upon which to build faith in later years.

For all of us raised in this tradition, prayer—or our methods of prayer—set us apart from others and grounded us in a tradition that we could trace back directly to Christ and the apostles, the ancient saints and the Church fathers. But I think that prayer in itself, communication between the human being and the Divine Being, is more or less the same in any tradition.

We can pray in the words of our church's tradition or we

can choose our own words. As long as the intention is heart-felt, as long as the need to be close to and communicate with God is expressed, then that is prayer. Even if we do not experience tangible, direct results from our prayers—especially if we do not get what we want—we gain a sense of spiritual well-being, even amid troubles. The key is to open the line of communication with God.

As adults, our prayer life is often mixed. Sometimes we turn from prayer. Why? The exigencies of daily life, forgetfulness, even anger at God are some reasons. I have found that if I do not adhere to a routine of spiritual reading, meditation, and prayer—for me, the early morning hours are best—then I lose that bond of communication and lose the comfort level that constant application sustains. Perhaps a crisis of faith has turned us away from God, from worship, from prayer, or from any spiritual exercise. This is common: the falling away and the return. It is purely a free and individual choice, to pray or not to pray.

So how do I—how do any of us—pray best? The answer is as varied as our experiences and the levels of our commitment to faith in a Higher Power. I find it most helpful to get down on my knees and assume the familiar position of respect before the Almighty Father. Many people I know pray when they are walking or driving. On the appointed day, in one's own house of worship, prayer comes more naturally and easily, perhaps. That's the time to go with it! In my mind, there is no wrong time, place, or method of prayer.

Don't worry about the words, especially if you have not prayed for a while. The simple attempt is worth more than a perfectly phrased paragraph.

Prayer

I ask, this day, for the willingness to open my heart to God, to speak what is in my mind, to give what is in my heart, and to listen to what God has to say to me in return: grant me the strength to be constant in prayer; grant me the strength to fall to my knees each day of my life to give praise and thanks. I ask, too, that You direct my prayers for others, that they may know the abundance of Your grace— that Your will, not mine, be done. Jesus, Son of the Father, hear my prayer.

THE GOSPEL

We ought to fish well and with diligent care, as the Lord commands and teaches, saying: "Follow Me, and I will make you fishers of men." Again He says through the prophets: "Behold, I send many fishers and hunters, says God," and so on.

This is why it was most necessary to spread our nets widely so that a great throng and multitude might be captured for God, and that there be clergy everywhere to baptize and teach a people who need and want so badly, as the Lord admonishes in the Gospel, saying: "Go now and teach all nations, baptizing them in the name of the Father and of the Son and of the Holy Spirit, teaching them to observe all the things I have taught you; and see, I am with you all days, even until the end of the world." And again He says: "Go out therefore to the whole world and preach the gospel to every creature. He who believes and is baptized shall be saved, but he who does not believe shall be condemned." And again: "This gospel of the kingdom shall be preached in the

*entire world for a testimony to all races of people, and then shall
the end come." And so, too, the Lord announces through the
prophet, and says: "And it shall come to pass, in the last days,
says the Lord, I will pour out my Spirit upon all flesh, and your
sons and your daughters shall prophesy, and your young men
shall see visions, and your old ones shall dream dreams. And
upon my manservants and maidservants I will pour out my
Spirit, and they, too, shall prophesy."*

*Finally, in Hosea He says: "I will call those who were not
My people, My people; and those who have not received My
mercy, they shall receive My mercy. And where before in the
place where it was said, 'You are not my people,' there they shall
be called children of the living God."*

[*CONFESSION*, CH. **40**]

Commentary

Patrick believed the Gospel, loved the Gospel, and
preached the Gospel unceasingly during his ministry to the
Irish. He took seriously Christ's invitation to the first
apostles: "Follow Me, and I will make you fishers of men!"
What more exhilarating or higher calling was there, in the
end times, as Rome crumbled and the day of the Redeemer's coming to judge the living and the dead loomed
ever nearer? Patrick fit the apostolic mold because he abandoned everything—even "traded my birthright," he reminds
us at one point in the *Letter*. He left the presumed comfort
of his home and the bosom of his kinsmen (although we do
not know for certain whether his parents survived into his
adult years) who begged him to stay with them.

He chose the way of Christ as found in the canonical
Gospels of the first apostles.

Like many of the prophets of the Hebrew Bible and John the Baptizer and St. Paul of the New Testament, Patrick's belief in his Lord was like a deep well, which he drew from in times of adversity. In his case, a profound faith followed a period of unbelief as a very young man, before his years of captivity. He subsequently turned to God on the cold hillside and found Him there; in fact, He had always been within Patrick's own heart, a small, still voice that the youth did not, or chose not, to hear. Yet, when he was struck, like Saul of Tarsus, with the lightning bolt of faith and heard the voice of God, he was never the same again; his path was set before him from that moment.

Like Jonah to Nineveh or Christ to Jerusalem, he set out on a perilous journey with the word of God as his only familiar. True, he had some followers—an army by some legendary accounts; more likely, it was a small staff of priests and helpers. So Patrick was not completely alone as some of the ancient prophets had been. But it was a lonely road nonetheless, for on his shoulders lay the sacerdotal burden of his office. The people would look to him alone to represent the authority of the foreign-based Church in their land. And he took the responsibility seriously: it was something he had sought, despite setbacks and misgivings, and he would not shirk such a burden nor walk away from the people who had called him back to walk among them.

Patrick had studied long and hard during his years of priestly formation—whether in Gaul or Britain or elsewhere; we can never know for certain—learning to employ his admittedly rudimentary language skills in pursuit of sacred ends. We don't know what kind of student, but I would hazard a guess that he was the earnest, awkward type who stumbled academically but soared spiritually. We cannot doubt that he maintained his habit of constant prayer, perhaps to the dismay or amusement of fellow students.

He was different, this is clear. But he did not brook unorthodoxy, for he was armed with an abiding knowledge of Holy Scripture in the form of the Latin Bible. Therein were the words that could—and did—preserve him from his enemies and light the way for those who followed him. He was possessed of the knowledge that he could call upon God at any time to support him, and he held in his hands, in the Book, the power of the gospel to change men's hearts. He employed that power throughout his long and successful ministry.

He could also look to Scripture for historical precedent for—and solutions to—his own troubles with the opponents of his mission, both among the native Irish and back home in Britain.

St. Patrick, as we have seen elsewhere in this study, never doubted the message of his Savior. As the bishop says in the *Confession*, Christ "never disappoints." [ch. 39] From Patrick's constant study of the New Testament he grew ever more steadfast in his faith; he found all his answers there, for he believed without reservation in the Christlike way of life. What more need he know when God's plan was so clearly laid out?

Time was of the essence, as well. There just wasn't very much left, or so it was believed at the time; he had to get out to the Irish "nation" and teach them and baptize them. He was a fisher and a hunter who spread his net widely to capture the maximum number of souls for God. The net consisted of priests whom he ordained to serve the missionary see of Ireland, for there were in the neighborhood of a half-million people living on the island in his time (according to de Paor). This was no small task, then, to preach and administer sacraments—all the while watching his backside for attacks from his home church in Britain.

Unmindful of heresies and internal controversies that swirled through the fifth-century church like locusts, Patrick hewed to the single, simple message of redemption through Jesus Christ as described in the four Gospels and the chronicles of the apostles following Christ's resurrection and ascension. On a day-by-day basis he moved from one house or overnight camp to the next, always seeking to win another soul, crying out in the literal wilderness in the words of those who had come before him, preaching and exhorting his listeners to change their ways, to accept a new life for a new, quickened age, to participate in the sacraments—before all must face the final judgment of the living and the dead in the impending last days.

Patrick's gospel is our gospel. He was wrong about the end of the world but right about the essentials of a system of morality and a revolutionary new way of life—based on the testament of his Savior that he knew to be true.

Contemplation

St. Patrick's homiletic ability is astoundingly evident in his writing. It is as if he is present with us, teaching us, urging us forward on the path to eternal glory. This is the essence of his apostolate: his stern but loving application of the Gospel in his own life.

What message does the Gospel hold for me today? Is it the same dynamic document of faith that Patrick found it to be? Do I listen when the Gospel is read to me; do I understand and apply the words when I read it for myself?

Has the Gospel entered my consciousness and infused me with the Spirit as it did to Patrick?

The answers to these questions are not as obvious as they may at first seem. The sticking point is me: the message is available at a moment's notice, if I choose to seek it. I am by nature a seeker after community and knowledge; this is my humanity. But I am also naturally resistant to that which is not tangible, not evident as real. No matter that I am familiar with miracles in real life—the small but significant transformation of people, myself included—it seems that I must learn and relearn the basic lesson ad nauseum.

To me the Gospel is a great adventure story: the progress of a young man who became the greatest Teacher we have ever known. His earthly life was brief and tragic, yet it is the most powerful lesson we have of God's power to save any of us in our wretched human condition. Like Patrick's life, the whole biography of Jesus of Nazareth is not knowable to us, but there is ample evidence of his ministry in the canon of Matthew, Mark, Luke, and John. These Gospels give us the barest outline of a life and an irresistible message of hope. They tell of miracles and parables and journeyings through Palestine (which was at that time an imperial province just four hundred years before Patrick's time). The Gospel (singular) is, then, the codified text of Jesus' time on earth and the basis for the teachings of Patrick's church.

I receive comfort and healing from the message of the Gospel. Through the apostolic tradition that has existed for two thousand years, the priests and bishops have preserved and carried this message, interpreted and implemented it, kept it alive for me and my family to benefit from the Spirit therein. The simplicity of Christ's teaching penetrates time and the accretion of man-made traditions. His Word is pure, straightforward, understandable, applicable to contemporary daily life. He speaks directly to me, as long as I am attuned to His teaching.

Like the apostles of old—and like Patrick in his time—the preachers and churchmen of our day are the hunters and fishers of men; they are the shepherds who seek the lost ones at Christ's direction. They seek to bring you and me into the fold where the Great Shepherd will tend to our needs and keep us safe. I respect this evangelical effort and must maintain an open-minded attitude toward those imperfect messengers who, though they may err and stumble, do so in the service of their fellow men.

The Gospel is not a cure-all, but it certainly is effective medicine. Sometimes it is difficult for me to swallow, but I always feel better afterward. Here is another example of how, when I get out of my own way and become an open channel for communication with my Creator, I reap spiritual benefits beyond my means and deserts. My way (self-focused, wrongheaded, sometimes even harmful to myself and others) leads nowhere; His way, as expressed in the gospel message, leads to happiness and fulfillment in the kingdom.

Prayer

Father, let me learn to listen so that I may listen to learn Your will for me. Teach me to heed the Word, that I may know the way of life You intend for me. Lead me to the water of life that I may drink deeply and become infused with Your power and Your love. The path is before me; the map is available to me; I pray that I may put one foot in front of the other and strike out in the right direction—toward you.

FAITH

And there one night in my sleep I heard a voice saying to me: "It is good that you fast, for soon you will return to your own country." And once again, after a short time I heard the voice tell me: "Come see, your ship is ready." But it was not near. It lay at a distance of perhaps two hundred miles away, and I had never been there, nor did I know a living soul there. Soon after, I took to flight and left behind the man to whom I had been a bond servant for six years. And I traveled with the strength of God who directed my way successfully, and I feared nothing until I reached that ship.

And the very day that I arrived at the harbor the ship was setting to sea, and I said that I was able to pay for my passage with them. But the captain was angry, and he answered my request harshly: "It is of no use for you to ask us to go along with us!" When I heard this, I turned and left them to return to the hut where I was staying. And as I walked away, I began to pray; and before I had even ended my prayer I heard one of them shouting behind me, "Come, hurry, we shall take you on board in good faith. . . ."

In three days we made landfall, and we journeyed for twenty-eight days through a deserted, barren wilderness. No food was to be found and hunger overcame them. One day the captain turned to me and said, "What do you say, Christian? You claim that your God is great and powerful. So why don't you pray for us? For we are in immediate danger of starving; we may not live to see another human being ever again." Then I said confidently [and calmly] to them: "Trust with all your hearts in the Lord my God—for Him nothing is impossible—so that this day He may send you enough food for your journey until you are satisfied. For He has abundance everywhere."

By the hand of God, so it came to pass. Suddenly, right before our eyes, a herd of swine appeared on the road. The crew killed many of them and spent two nights there, and were refreshed and recovered their strength. Their hounds were also fed and revived, for many of them had also become weak with hunger and were left to die by the side of the road. And after this, the men gave much thanks to God, and I became highly esteemed in their eyes. There was food in great abundance from that day forward. They even found wild honey and offered me a taste of it. But then I heard one of them say, "May this be a sacrifice to our gods." Thanks be to the true God, I tasted none of it.

[CONFESSION, CH. 17–19]

Commentary

Early in his long life, Patrick, by his own account, had fallen away from Church teaching and lived without any focus on God. We cannot know for certain how devout his father and mother were, for despite his father's diaconate, the author of the *Confession* and the *Letter* tells us little about them. Perhaps Sucatus (or Sucat) was simply a rebellious boy, as boys often are. Was his a conscious rejection of Jesus, or merely a careless tossing away of his Christian faith tradition? Did he argue with his parents or grandfather, refuse to attend mass, ignore his religious obligations altogether? We can imagine him in this period of his youth as perhaps restless, rambunctious, physical, materialistic, immature, eager to see the wider world, to be on his own.

I suspect that he knew a childish faith as a very young boy, and that he was well-taught as to the expectations that were placed on the shoulders of a Christian lad who had sprung from such a rich tradition of service to the Church. Therefore, it was all the more significant for Patrick to put aside his Christian faith—for whatever the reason.

Then—he reclaimed it! Haunted, perhaps, by the mortal sin he committed as a youth (and confessed, years later, on the eve of his taking holy orders) and taken against his will into servitude in a wild, foreign land, the teenager who had rejected the Christian faith for earthly pleasure turned his face and his heart to God in his time of need. And God answered him, resoundingly.

In the passage that tells the story of his escape from enslavement, Patrick relates a series of events that required him to follow God's direction through one impossible situation after another. First, he had to leave his place of captivity without being caught. Then he traveled two hundred miles through alien country, only to be refused passage on the ship that came to him in his dream. Patrick swallows his pride, turns away, prays for help—and is rewarded with a change of heart. The voyage among strangers with their strange cargo—Irish wolfhounds, we think—could not have been easy for him. Then landfall: and the party wandered through a "desert" and nearly starved, until—when challenged by his heathen comrades—Patrick summons yet another miracle through prayer: a herd of wild pigs crosses their path, and they can eat.

Time after time, as shown in this brief passage, young Patrick's spiritual mettle was tested; time after time, he trusted God and followed His promptings. He took the next step forward—and he followed a path of miracles that took him to freedom and a new life.

This pattern recurred throughout his life. Patrick developed a close relationship with the God of his family's Church; his God became a personal presence and guide, a supporter and supplier of strength. He invested his belief, as we see elsewhere, in the Holy Trinity, which he preached with enthusiasm to the thousands whom he would baptize as a missionary bishop. God led, and Patrick followed. God sent a vision, and Patrick obeyed. God stirred Patrick's heart, and the man prayed for grace and the ability to follow God's will.

His faith was not simply a matter of belief, and it was in no way passive or static. Patrick's was an engaged faith that grew as his life unfolded. He sought to believe more deeply, challenged himself, and tested himself. And God was always there to answer his prayers, to show him the way.

When he was called by the Irish in the famous dream, he knew in his heart—there was no doubt whatsoever—

that the calling was true, and that this was his life's work. In order to accomplish the work, however, he faced many obstacles—not the least of which, apparently, was resistance in the British Church to his candidacy for bishop. For reasons unknown, Patrick was not the first man chosen for the apostolate to the Irish people; instead, Palladius was named to found the mission in Hibernia. This no doubt irritated and disappointed Patrick who, from his perspective during that time of his life, had been preparing for this calling for many years. Again, he was compelled to fall back on his faith when men failed him—or when God had determined that the time was not right.

What else was there to do but dig deeper, put aside his pride, accept God's will?

St. Patrick was a practical man, as well as a mystic. He sought results from his actions, expected a lot of himself and from God. He was willing to do the footwork and to pray without ceasing. He acquired, over many years, a quality of faith that was unshakable. This faith required a sacrifice of self, a complete trust in God. This was an active, not a passive faith; it was a virtue that found flower in doing more than believing. The true miracles in Patrick's life followed—rather than preceded—his leap into faith.

Contemplation

What is the quality of my faith? Not the quantity. For if I were to measure my faith by quantity, I might come up to a thimbleful, little more.

It is a mystery to me why this should be. After all, I, too, have experienced miracles and manifestations of God in my own life; and I have seen Him work in others' lives, as well. I have been educated in the faith tradition of my fathers that, in fact, reaches back directly to St. Patrick himself. I pray and worship and meditate upon the nature of God. I am surrounded by people of faith: in my family, in my parish community, among my friends and colleagues.

How, then, can I possibly waver in my faith or entertain any doubts about the Supreme Source of all that is good and positive in my life? The answer is simple: I am human. I have the ability to make my life more difficult and complicated than it need be.

I am grateful that God can accept my humanity; after all, He is the Author of that book. So, my task, in the quest for an increase in faith is, first, to accept my condition, then to work daily to reclaim the childlike condition of utter trust in my Creator. I must follow St. Patrick's example of steadfastness; he never relinquished hope, never lost faith, never stopped praying for guidance. His life of hardship and danger only reinforced his faith in God, and he was never reluctant to offer yet another sacrifice to his Father.

My mission is perhaps less urgent than Patrick's, yet I often feel that I face impossible responsibilities. The pressures of our world are intense and very real. Yet there is relief. I know this. I know that when I take the time to be quiet and to contemplate God's goodness, I experience immediate relief and renewed energy to face the grinding tasks of a given day. With an attitude of faith—that there is an ultimate purpose to my being here and a meaning to the relationships in my life—everything in the human realm is made manageable.

Faith is more than belief; it is more than a cardinal virtue. *Faith is a way of life*. Faith is a partnership of God with the individual. Faith is a result of prayer and hard spiritual work and, in turn, makes prayer and spiritual work possible. It is a mystery and it makes all things clear. By holding faith up to the light, by examining my relationship with God in this light, I am able to increase the measure and the quality of faith in my life. Day by day my cup—my thimble—overflows with faith, if I hold it up to Him with a receptive heart.

Prayer

I pray, Heavenly Father, for the quality of faith that St. Patrick possessed in such great measure. He believed that he had a purpose in this world of woes; he believed with a vivid purity that allowed no room for doubt. May I be given such faith that will sustain me in difficult times, illuminate my thoughts about God, give me strength and conviction in human relationships. Fill me up with faith, Heavenly Father, that I may believe in Your goodness and be of service to others.

Unconditional Love

or that sun, which we see rising every day, rises at His command; but it will never rule over the universe, nor will its splendor last forever. And all those who worship it will end in misery and receive terrible punishment. But not we, who believe in and worship the true sun, Christ; He shall never die, and neither will anyone who does His will—instead he shall live forever, just as Christ lives forever, who reigns with God the Father Almighty and with the Holy Spirit since before the beginning of time and forever after. Amen.

[*Confession*, CH. 60]

Commentary

St. Patrick preached the Holy Trinity in a sincere, direct way that put it within the grasp of the very simplest of those whom he sought to bring to Christ. He accepted the orthodoxy of the ancient Christian Church and rejected any heresy that arose—as many did before and during his lifetime. He also revered the Holy Bible, which, in the vulgar Latin version he knew, contained for him every jot of "book knowledge" that he required. He especially loved the New Testament Gospels and the epistles of St. Paul, whom he quotes throughout his extant writings. The Scripture was his bulwark, his foundation, his life. Even as he counted himself ignorant and uneducated, he possessed a visceral and intellectual grasp of the essentials of Christian faith that might still be the envy of any contemporary theologian.

The Apostle of Ireland cherished the Passion of Christ and incorporated its meaning into his own life's mission. In each of the synoptic Gospels of Matthew, Mark, and Luke, as well as the Gospel of John, the Passion of Jesus is described in some detail: from the night of prayer in Gethsemane to His betrayal and arrest to His interrogation, torture, and death. Each Gospel adds information and interpretation to the story, so that we have received a fairly complete picture of the events of those hours after the Last Supper and before the burial. For Patrick, the person of Jesus who "was crucified, died, and was buried," was the most immediately accessible component of the Trinity. The Passion of Christ bonded the human Jesus to men of later generations; His intense suffering prefigures our own, and His resurrection and His eternal life with the Father is likewise promised to each of us.

While the Gospel story of Jesus of Nazareth has the ultimate "happy ending" (i.e., resurrection and ascension into heaven), there are some rather gruesome and tragic aspects of the latter chapters of Jesus' life. These historical events we learn in just enough detail to leave our imaginations (or that of artists through the centuries) plenty of room to maneuver. Upon His entry into Jerusalem, Jesus entered a death trap. As the story unfolds, He violently confronts the merchants and money changers in the temple; He enjoys a Passover seder with His closest disciples, where He predicts that one of them, Judas, will betray Him; He goes to pray in a garden and feels as alone as anyone possibly can, and asks that God take away the cup (the impending self-sacrifice); He castigates the apostles who fell asleep as He was praying; He is arrested and taken into custody, passed from local authorities after a disruptive hearing before the Sanhedrin into Roman hands, stripped and tortured, brought before the procurator Pilate, who then "washes his hands" of the problem and sends Jesus to His death by crucifixion. The spiral continues downward, as the man from Nazareth carries His cross through the streets of Jerusalem to the hill of execution, where He is affixed to the wooden cross, and there, after three hours, He dies. Some bargaining thereafter secures permission for His followers to take His body to burial.

There are moments that are seared into the brain of anyone who has listened to the Passion read or who has walked the Stations of the Cross. Jesus' face is captured on Veronica's veil in a moment of kindness, as she wipes his brow of blood and sweat. Simon of Cyrene, a stranger, is pulled from the crowd of onlookers to help Him carry the heavy crossbeam that symbolizes His doom—another act of human kindness given Him. On the cross the dying Nazarene utters the words of forgiveness, "for they know not what they do," and gives comfort to the thief who is also dying on a nearby cross. And in His final surrender, before the knot of onlookers that includes His own mother,

Jesus finally and willingly gives up His spirit to His Father in heaven.

To the people who heard Patrick tell this story of sacrifice and redemption, it was a startling revelation: that an all-powerful God in heaven should manifest Himself on earth in the form of a beloved Son, for our sakes. The bishop-evangelist was not reluctant to leverage their awe and fascination; as we have learned, he converted them with alacrity and in large numbers. We might imagine that it was not only the story itself, but the power of the saint's testimony that persuaded so many Irish to put aside their long-held religious beliefs and be baptized in the Christian Church.

Bloodshed, torture, and pain were, one assumes, well known to these people whose beautiful, fertile land was a near-constant battlefield for warring kings and fierce clan leaders. This was the state of the world, to be accepted and suffered without question by the general population. There were, as we have stated before, no established cities (Dublin, for example, would not begin to coalesce as a town of any size until the Viking incursions of the ninth and tenth centuries) or fixed population centers other than within kingly redoubts that were built primarily for defensive purposes. And although there were artisans and farmers and soldiers, there was no class structure per se other than the aristocracy of kings and warriors—and everyone else.

Patrick's message leveled such distinctions as there were. Jesus Christ, we hear him preach, came to save the souls of all men and women throughout the world—even the Gentiles who lived at the ends of the earth. How did He do this? Through His teaching, His suffering, His death, and His resurrection. Why did He do this? Because He loved us as brethren, as fellow children of the Almighty Father. And what does He expect of us? To follow His example and love one another and be willing to lay down our lives—as Patrick clearly was—for a brother, or in the cause of truth. Patrick, who suffered his own trials (as evidenced in the *Confession* and the *Letter*, held up the Passion of Christ as the ultimate manifestation of God's unconditional love for each and all of us.

Contemplation

In childhood, the story of the Passion, which is recounted in the Gospel readings throughout Holy Week—the lead-up to the paschal celebration of Easter—is illustrative of Christ's humanity, humility, and final sacrifice of self.

Our personal trials and day-to-day sufferings pale in comparison to the story of the Passion. Often we get caught up in our own misery and discomfort; sometimes we cause our own problems. Sometimes our problems are not that serious, except when life itself is at stake through severe illness or accident or sudden death. There are degrees of personal suffering, which is not meant to minimize any of them for any individual. Then, there is public or global suffering: famines, wars, genocide, tyranny, injustice, natural disasters. Our hearts go out to the victims of these events, and our own troubles then take on different proportions. Our moral training and instincts tell us to pray for others who are suffering, whatever the cause and wherever they may be.

We often describe personal suffering as "my cross to bear." This phrasing comes, of course, from the experience of the Passion. In this situation it is difficult to look up and see the sun rising, to contemplate the persons of the Trinity, to see beyond the immediate physical or emotional pain. Yet God wishes us to be happy, not to suffer—or else, to be able to alleviate our suffering through His grace and the love of other people.

When I bear my cross, I must stop and look up and ask for help. As difficult as it may be, I must step out of myself, away from my isolation. In God, through other people in my life, I will find relief, solace, comfort, healing. Perhaps I cannot live a life that's problem-free, but I can better handle life on life's terms with help.

St. Paul, in his epistle addressed to the Hebrews, writes: "Let us keep our eyes fixed on Jesus, on whom our faith depends from beginning to end. He did not give up because of the cross! On the contrary, because of the joy that was waiting for him, he thought nothing of the disgrace of dying on the cross, and is now seated at the right side of God's throne." [Hebrews 12:2]

The One who suffered this deepest humiliation for all of us was heedless of the shame in the tawdry, criminal circumstance of His own death. Why? Because He knew that the Father awaited Him with a crown of glory to replace the crown of thorns. And to believers, who are admonished by Paul to keep their eyes firmly fixed on the example of His Passion as the basis of faith, there is the assurance that this very day Christ sits with the Father and the Holy Spirit and calls each of us to join Him there.

I do not invite suffering into my life; in fact, I resist it and pray that I and my loved ones are spared suffering. In the past, with the illness and passing of parents, the disappointments in the workplace, the personal failures and humiliation in relationships, the fact of others' sickness and need, the feelings of inadequacy and unworthiness—with all these things and more, I am still standing today. Perhaps it is just for today, and tomorrow will bring new sorrows and defeats. I do not control events and other people, and I cannot know when I shall face the next difficult challenge. What I do know is that I am called to be spiritually fit to meet any challenge. I am called to be like Christ in this way.

How will I respond to the call—freely and faithfully, without fear? This I know: I will prepare to serve my Father and my fellow man, even unto death, for He has a plan for me that I cannot comprehend except as it unfolds one day at a time.

The Passion not only teaches me, but empowers me: it is the ultimate demonstration of God's unconditional love for me and for others. I draw strength and inspiration from the example of Christ's sacrifice and from His Father's undying love for the Son of Man. The imitation of Christ is the act of living a life of love and sacrifice—imperfect though any human attempt may be.

Prayer

Father, I pray that I may learn the chief lesson of life from the Passion of Jesus Christ: that You love me without stint or condition. I pray that His example of courage and willingness will inspire me to act in a way befitting Your child in times of trial. Grant me the strength to go from here on my mission, whatever that may be, willing to face what comes. If I am called upon to make such a sacrifice for Your sake, or the sake of a brother, help me to see it through.

GRIEF

I do not know what more I should say or how I can speak of those dead children of God who were ruthlessly struck down by the sword. For it is written: "Weep with those who weep." And again: "If one member grieves, let all be sorrowful." Therefore the entire Church weeps and mourns her sons and daughters whom the sword has not yet touched [slain], but who were made into slaves and taken to distant lands where terrible sin abounds, openly, wickedly, and without shame. Freeborn men are sold there and Christians enslaved—and, worst of all, they are sold to the most despicable and apostate Picts.

For this reason I cry aloud in sadness and grief: O most beautiful and beloved brothers and sons whom I confirmed in Christ, and whom I cannot number, what shall I do for you now? I am unworthy to help either God or man. The injustice of wicked men has overcome us. It has made us strangers to one another. Perhaps they do not believe that we have received the same baptism, or that we have the same God and the same Father. They look down at us because we are Irish. But the prophet said: "Have you not the one God? Why have you—each and every one of you—forsaken your neighbor?"

Consequently, I grieve for you. Indeed, I deeply mourn for you, my dearly beloved ones. Yet, I also rejoice within myself. For I see that I have not labored without result, and my journey [exile] to an alien land was not without purpose. And though this was an unspeakably horrible crime, I thank God that you were baptized believers when you left this world for paradise. I can see you in a vision: you have embarked upon your journey to a place where there is no more night, no sorrow, and no death. Freed from your chains, you will romp like young lambs and the wicked will be like ashes beneath your feet.

[LETTER, CH. 15–17]

Commentary

The entire *Letter to the Soldiers of Coroticus* is an anguished cry of grief. Here, however, is the heart of the matter, as Patrick addresses directly those young Christians who were murdered and those who were captured, the dead and the living. Representing the Church, the entire Body of Christ, the community of believers in Ireland, St. Patrick weeps loudly and long over the loss of these "children of God" who have been taken from his care, who are separated from their brethren through no fault of their own except, perhaps, that they were in the wrong place at the wrong time. It is especially abhorrent to him that the innocents who still live have been taken to places of sin and corruption, made slaves to apostates who hate the gospel and the Church. They are the victims of evil men.

As for the dead, they were taken from the earth unjustly, shockingly, all too suddenly. Even in a world of violence, which the fifth century undoubtedly was, their slaughter was cause for intense anger and grief by Bishop Patrick. His love, that of a pastor and shepherd, is deep and undying. Like a father, he mourns from the depths of his heart his children who have passed before him.

He grieves for the living, too. After all, they are in the worst condition of all: imprisoned and enslaved, sold and bartered. He lavishes his love on them and deems them as precious as his own children, for they are indeed his spiritual progeny. From here it seems clear that Patrick was not thinking only of the effect the *Letter* would have on the soldiers. He was thinking of the many listeners to public readings of the *Letter*, and it was probably the case that the document was read widely in both Britain and Ireland.

This might explain the odd sentence in chapter 16 that puzzles the commentators: "They look down at us because we are Irish." Patrick was not Irish, but British, yet here he confirms that he has taken on the identity of the people of his ministry. Elsewhere Patrick reminds us that he sold or traded his birth status as a Roman Briton; he continually claims to be an exile, never to be reunited with his kin and countrymen. Always he seems to have them—and his clerical elders in Britain—in mind as he writes. Not only, then, was the *Letter* read throughout the British Isles, but an even wider, more distant audience. Patrick may, in the immediate picture, be excommunicating Coroticus and his band, but they are largely beyond talking to; it is probably too late for them to come back to the faith.

But, having brought the gospel to the very edge of the earth (of that time), Patrick sees his mission as the final victory of Christianity in Europe. We do not know the outcome of his contest of wills with Coroticus, and we have every reason to fear the worst for the captives. Nonetheless, Patrick is serving notice that his has been a greater victory. The bringing of the word of God to Ireland—and infusing such an intensity that its glow endures so many centuries later—means for Patrick that all of Europe has become a part of the kingdom of heaven. The history of Christianity has been birthed; its raucous youth and adolescence now begins.

There is joy, painful and bittersweet, even in this time of intense grieving. The bishop gropes for words to communicate these mixed emotions and finds, as he does throughout his writings, what he requires in his Bible. His prophetic power is fueled by the words of prophets and apostles who came before him. It is perfectly appropriate for him to do so since he is no rhetorician himself. But, as we see elsewhere, his deep emotion brings out the most creative and evocative language that he is capable of. "Freed from your chains," he says of the baptized Christians who were murdered, "you will romp like young lambs and the wicked will be like ashes beneath your feet." He reaffirms the rewards that await those who die in communion with Jesus.

He goes on to say, in part, in chapter 18 of the *Letter*: "You will reign with the apostles and the prophets and the martyrs. You will win eternal kingdoms, just as He Himself promised: 'They shall come from the east and west, and they shall sit with Abraham, Isaac, and Jacob in the kingdom of heaven.'"

Grief had been a familiar companion to Patrick since his time of captivity, the loss of his parents, the betrayal of his best friend, separation from his native land. Rarely has the emotion and its spiritual resonance been so convincingly communicated.

Contemplation

I know of no one who has not experienced grief, some more intimately or more immediately than others. Just look around and you will see in your circle of family and friends, and in your own life, examples. Recently, two close colleagues of mine lost their mothers to age and illness; accidents and violence have claimed friends; my own parents died when I was relatively young (in my twenties and early thirties), but their passing still leaves a gaping hole in my life that is difficult to fill—or to understand.

The loss of a friendship or a job is also cause to grieve. Embarrassment due to an error or immature action may be cause to grieve. Tragic public events such as death and assassination, crimes in high places, the absence of honorable leadership, deception by and disappointment in one-time heroes or celebrities are all cause for grief by some, perhaps ridicule or revilement by others. Grief is a very personal, intimate reaction that is not always shared equally and universally.

From Patrick we can glean some important lessons. First, it is important to acknowledge, indeed to proclaim our grief. "Weep with those who weep." I would add, Do not hold back the emotion caused by the loss. As I age and mature I find that I need to cry now and then; it is cleansing and healthy for me. Sometimes the cause may be rather trivial—a sentimental movie—or more profound: I remember the heavy tears at the funeral of a young friend who had been killed in a freak motorbike accident, leaving a wife and two very small children. Like anger and other sometimes overpowering emotions, grief demands an outlet. I believe that tears are a God-given remedy that relieves the mourner and joins him with the human race.

Second, grief reminds us that there is purpose and value in the life of human beings. Why are we so deflated in the moment of loss? It is not purely a selfish reaction; we truly feel the diminishment in our own lives when another passes away. We gain our humanity through our bond with others—first and most strongly, our parents and siblings and other family members. As we grow and expand our circle of acquaintances and relationships, we take steps ever closer to other men and women. When we attempt, as Patrick did, to influence others—as parents ourselves, as teachers, as salesmen and advocates—we cement the bond even more tightly. We increase our investment daily in the lives of others. Therefore, when another is taken from us, we truly know that not only the quantity but the quality of life itself—earthly, mortal life—has been reduced. And we are powerless to change that; we can only learn to accept and deal with it.

A third lesson we can draw from Patrick is that faith triumphs over every adversity, no matter how painful. Prayer and worship, along with the rituals of mourning, remind us of the well-worn adage, "Life goes on." It does—for the living. But for the faithful, in the Christian and other traditions, so does life continue for those who have been taken from mortal existence. In the case of the martyrs about whom Patrick writes in the *Letter*, they were so freshly baptized that they still wore the white garments of the ceremony and the chrism, or anointing oil, was still gleaming on their foreheads. They were taken, in Patrick's belief, to feast with the fathers of the chosen people in the kingdom of heaven. The murderers and blasphemers, Patrick believes, are damned to the lake of eternal fire. So, grief may be mitigated by the notion that the just are rewarded for their good actions and may await us—we who are earthbound and "prisoners of the flesh."

Each day I experience a bit of grief for the day just past, for deeds undone, for wrongs committed, for the absence of ones I love. Yet, intermingled with and despite that sorrow is a joy in the gift of life itself. This is what it means to be human.

Prayer

In times of sadness and loss, please stand by my side, Heavenly Father. I need Your presence and Your arms; embrace me and comfort me as You have comforted Your people from time immemorial. I give myself up to You, and I let go of my self-concerns and self-centeredness. I trust You to take care of each of Your children, living and dead. I look to You in every moment of every day, in good times and bad.

A SERVANT
OF GOD

So therefore I, at once a rustic and an exile, unlearned, who does not know how to provide for the future—this at least I know with complete certainty that before I was humiliated I was like some big stone lying deep in the mud; and He who is all-powerful came and in His mercy lifted me up and raised me aloft to a place on the very top of the wall. Therefore I should cry out aloud and so also render something back to the Lord for His great benefits here and throughout eternity—gifts that the simple mind of man is unable to comprehend.

For this reason then, be astounded, all of you great and small who fear God, and you men of rhetoric on your estates, listen and pay attention to this. Who was it that raised me up, fool that I am, from among those who in the eyes of men are considered wise and expert in the law and powerful in speech and in everything? And He inspired me—me, a despised outcast of this world—above many others, to be the man (if only I could!) who, with reverence and without complaint, should faithfully serve the race of Gentiles to whom the love of Christ brought me and left me for the remainder of my life, if I should be so worthy; yes, to serve them humbly and sincerely.

[*CONFESSION*, CH. 12–13]

Commentary

A resounding theme of Patrick's life and work is service to God. His relationship with God seems to have been a very direct one, maintained through a rigorous prayer life and an openness to the Father's communication with him in dreams and visions. On a practical and earthly level, he served his Lord through his ceaseless missionary activities: proselytizing, baptizing, confirming, ordaining clergy, bringing the gospel to the people "to whom the love of Christ brought me." God, in turn, blessed the saint's service with spiritual benefits that were, according to St. Patrick's own account, incalculable and not understandable or describable in human terms.

The legendary lives of St. Patrick imputed miraculous powers to Patrick throughout his life. Consistent with other evidence, the legendary Patrick often employs these miracles in the service of others and to prove God's power and love to those who did not believe. If we discount any venal or narrow motives that inflict pain or punishment on wicked people whom he might have encountered, which many of the later myths illustrate, we are left with the assumption that any miracles he may have performed were with a pure, God-loving heart for the good of his fellow men. I have little doubt that Patrick did perform miracles in the course of his long and prodigiously successful evangelizing career.

In fact, no man has ever loved God more than Patrick. With every fiber of his being, he credits the Creator in the documents with the supreme power to make or break him. This love, along with a powerful faith and an equally unwavering commitment to service, sustains Patrick in everything he does, miracle or no.

He imputes no malign motive to God even when he is made low in the eyes of his fellow men, humiliated. He is too imperfect and unselfish a vessel not to fail constantly, to let down those who expect great things of him, to incite jealousy for his successes, to make mistakes and missteps. For Patrick knows that through faithful service and striving for the right, he will be lifted up and rewarded at the end. Even in his lifetime, despite the troubles that he experienced (as, of course, we all do) he tells us that he reaped the rewards of ceaseless service to the cause of Christ.

Elsewhere in the *Confession* and the *Letter*, Patrick recounts the positive, tangible results of his hard work in service to God. He baptized the Irish by the thousands. When the armies of Coroticus rape and slaughter and enslave young Christians who still wear the chrism of confirmation on their foreheads, Patrick is wild with grief and anger. Not his efforts, but the will of God, has been thwarted by evil men. Thus Patrick is unafraid to threaten damnation and excommunication for their actions, for that is God's will: that His children not be violated. Patrick, servant and messenger, condemns these wrong actions. He is not afraid to do right, even when it is difficult or painful—or dangerous.

The metaphor that St. Patrick employs in the above-quoted passage from the *Confession* is one of the most powerful and beautiful in all of his writings. He tells us that he was as low as any human being could be, like an inert, lifeless stone stuck in the mud, unable to see or feel the sun, unknown, unloved, and incapable of love. I picture a gray, drizzly day on a grassless plain, perhaps near one of the old walls constructed by the Roman soldiers in the hinterlands of Britain, now abandoned as the empire collapsed. He was a self-admitted outcast, a pariah to some, loathed by others, looked upon with suspicion by still others. It is possible that he was feared and hated by some of the druid priesthood for threatening their very existence. Even if we allow for some small measure of rhetorical exaggeration, we can see that Patrick was a polarizing figure both within the British Church hierarchy and among the non-Christian people of Ireland to whom he was bound in service for the main part of his adult life. Similarly, Patrick had been bound as a slave and servant in his youth: then he had been a sheep or pig herder; and he had not had a choice, for he had been captured and indentured against his will.

So, Patrick is an insignificant piece of rock. He is buried in the muck and mire of earth, trampled beneath the feet of men, lower than the animals, less than the plants. He has no life, no purpose, no identity.

In an act of mercy, then, God, "He who is all-powerful," and He who is most merciful, raised the stone and placed it on top of the wall. There, the rain might wash the dirt and mud from the surface of the stone and smooth it and expose it to the light of the day yet to come. Atop the wall— again, the wonderful idea of an ancient defensive structure conjures a majestic image in the mind—the stone is now in the open, receptive to sunlight, visible to men. Perhaps it can be made useful: to repair the wall itself, to become part of a hearth or cooking circle, to be a weapon to defeat an enemy, to be a tool to build or tear down another structure.

We have every reason to be astonished, as Patrick says we ought to be. This God of his is capable of raising a fool and ignoramus to a position above the rest of us for a distinct purpose: to preach and convert the unbelievers. But Patrick displayed no foolishness at all in his hard-charging willingness to execute God's will. He was willing to be the best servant he could be, to put himself in danger, to spend the rest of his life in the strange place known as Ireland without hope of seeing his family and home ever again. These are incredible sacrifices; in Patrick's world, the so-called Dark Ages, there was no turning back on such a decision. It was as final as it could get. After all, according to his understanding, he had come to the last place on earth where the Word could have an effect.

So, Patrick trod the paths and hills of an alien land in service to God and man; perhaps he had an entourage of sorts—whether he had arrived in Ireland with a phalanx of clergy and workers, as some accounts would have it, or virtually alone, with the intention to recruit priests and helpers along the way—to assist him. He showed others the way through his example of self-abnegation. He expected no rewards, yet experienced so many in his life and after his life was ended. After all, we honor him today for the work that he accomplished by putting God and his fellow men first, himself last.

Jesus, as Messiah, embraced our human form "as slave." Likewise, to Patrick, there was no higher calling than to be a servant of God and his fellow men.

Contemplation

When I look upon my life as an opportunity to serve others, nearly all of my problems in the realm of human relationships melt away and solutions fall into place. An attitude of service, as embodied by Patrick who was following the gospel precepts of Christ, calms and sustains me through periods of uncertainty: "What am I doing here, anyway?" When I place this attitude ahead of my own pride and ambition, I feel better, more whole, straighter, more able to face my responsibilities—which do not diminish as time goes by.

It makes sense to me—based on simple observation and experience— that we are put here to help each other. We are husbands and wives, sons and daughters, mothers and fathers, colleagues, friends, supervisors, teachers, students, customers, employees, and there is, I believe, a reason for our being here together. My service is for you and through you for God. Service joins us one to the other in a spiritual marriage of need and reciprocation.

As a matter of practicality, how can I be of service to God and my fellows? Opportunities arise each and every day, if I am open to them. These opportunities occur at home, at work, in my parish, and in the community at large.

I have a lot of work to do as a spouse, parent, and friend. These are the most immediate and important relationships in my life, my highest obligation to serve. Through my everyday actions, my example, my willingness to listen, my presence, I fulfill my responsibility. Do I really listen when my partner is trying to direct me to take care of some task around the house? Do I stop, take the time to guide my children and know what they are doing, what they need, what they are thinking—without browbeating or creating unrealistic expectations? Am I truly a part of family activities when we are together: meals, trips, church attendance, games, quiet moments that will never come again? Do I hear my friends and fulfill their needs when they have a simple request?

Without being harsh on myself or others, I can establish a set of reasonable expectations, based on past behavior and my ability to change, to improve. Like the proverbial Boy Scout who assists the elderly lady across the busy street, I can quietly seek out opportunities for service, or be aware of the needs within my immediate circle of relationships.

The task for me, or for any of us regular-sized mortals—that is, we who are not saints—is not on the same scale as it was for Patrick. Yet it exists in the very same way, I think: we have been given gifts and raised from the mire by a Hand unseen. Therefore, we ought to announce to the world, through our service to others, that the Lord is the primary source of all the benefits we enjoy—indeed, of our very lives.

Prayer

I ask that I may adopt an attitude of service to You and to others. Let me serve my family with love in my heart. Let me serve friends with my presence in their lives when they need me. Let me serve colleagues and coworkers with diligence and an open hand. I trust the results of my right actions to You. I need Your constant grace and guidance if I am to be Your servant. I pray that I may serve God and others so that I will have a measure of happiness and usefulness in my life on earth.

J u s t i c e

*T*herefore, I do not know for whom I should more rightly grieve. Should I weep for those who were killed or captured, or for those whom the devil has enslaved? For they will be bound along with him [Satan] to the eternal pains of hell, since one who commits a mortal sin is himself a slave and is called the son of Satan.

So let every God-fearing person know that those who murder their own families, who kill their brothers like ravening wolves, who devour the people of the Lord as they would eat bread—they are forever estranged from me and from my God, whose missionary I am. As is said, "The wicked have destroyed Your law, O Lord," the law that He has of late—and at the end of time—graciously sown so successfully in Ireland to become firmly established there with God's grace.

I make no false accusation. [I do not exceed my authority.] I am the one He has called and preordained to preach the gospel despite so many serious persecutions and even to the very ends

of the earth, and though the enemy shows his disdain for me
through the actions of the tyrant Coroticus, who fears neither
God nor the clergy, whom He has chosen and whom He has
granted the highest spiritual power to bind in heaven those
whom they bind on earth.

[LETTER, CH. 4–6]

Commentary

In this passage from the *Letter to the Soldiers of Coroticus* Patrick is making his intentions clear: his purpose is to excommunicate these wrongdoers. In the passages that immediately follow (chapters 7–9 of the *Letter*), Patrick prescribes how and why the wicked must be shunned by the righteous. He lists their wicked deeds as if in a bill of indictment. He is concrete and damning in his accusations. He means to forbid other Christians from conversing or conducting any business with them, and very specifically forbids fellow clerics from accepting offerings, tithes, or alms from them. It seemed to some scholars that Patrick might be intruding into the diocesan affairs of another bishop, otherwise, why not simply issue the statement to his own flock?

The problem raised by the passage becomes somewhat more vexing with the uncertainty about the opening sentence of chapter 6: "I make no false accusation," which, in a clarifying or alternate reading, could be, "I do not exceed my authority." In the latter case it is an apology to the Church authorities on whose province Patrick has intruded (since it was they who should have issued the decree). But as we have discussed elsewhere, it may also be the case that Patrick had a dual purpose in mind: extending the scope of his teaching authority beyond Hibernia so that in the course of accepting his excommunication of these soldiers, he is gaining standing and prestige in the eyes of his countrymen, Britons, or at least forcing the issue.

Some authors speak of these possible ulterior motives with a kind of embarrassed reserve, as if there is something unseemly about Patrick having such ambitions. But one of the remarkable aspects of Patrick's career, and one which comes through clearly in both the *Confession* and the *Letter*, is his willingness to take the long view and see his mission in the context of history. Patrick speaks in both documents of the "end of time" as if he expected his conversion of the Irish to be the culmination of the conversion of all of Europe—and hence, all of humanity. Many of his contemporaries must have felt the same way, especially subsequent to the fall of Rome at the hands of Alaric in 410 C.E. Thus there is an apocalyptic and universalist theme in Patrick's language and argument that transcends parochial concerns: he wants the soldiers and those who know them to respond to the heinous deed with the moral revulsion of the God-fearing, wherever they may be.

God's justice can sometimes be harsh. Patrick finally and formally and very publicly excommunicates the soldiers. He views the actions of the marauders as an affront not simply to his office and his Church, but as a chapter in the heavenly struggle for the souls of the men and women of Ireland (and, by extension, throughout the empire of Rome). He is the grieving but willing messenger of a just and angry God. He lived in a world when evil was very palpable—unfortunately, not unlike our world in the last century. He reacted viscerally to injustice; he accepted calumny against his own person more readily than evil perpetrated against his flock. In this case, the crime is so ugly that the judgment must be swift and all-encompassing. Hence, the harsh, powerful tone of the *Letter*. Ultimately, "God Himself will surely judge." [*Letter*, ch. 14] Patrick acknowledges this; he may be angry, and he may be right, but he is a human being.

Still, as an ordained bishop of the church, Patrick claims the spiritual authority to sanction Coroticus and his men as a right; it is the "highest spiritual power to bind in heaven those whom they [the clergy] bind on earth." A legitimate function of his mission is the administration of justice. He is, in modern parlance, a crime fighter when crimes are committed against his own sons and daughters in Christ. He cannot have enjoyed this heavy responsibility, as it ran against his tolerant moral grain: he was harder on himself than others. The severity of the offenses, however, required that he exercise such judicial power as he saw fit. If he did not condemn these godless thugs, who would?

Justice, in Patrick's context, was the moral responsibility of men who proclaimed a just God, as His representatives on earth.

Contemplation

Even as I judge others—which, as a human being I cannot help but doing—I put myself forward to be judged. Justice means fairness, balance. It means redress of wrongs and acknowledgment of right. Justice is an absence of the judgmental, a presence of judiciousness. How would I have others view me and treat me? Do I behave in the same way I would prescribe for others?

In the arena of public affairs, which has been the focus of moral debate of late, these aspects of justice have been much discussed. We talk about applying certain moral standards. We gauge the meanings of sin, repentance, punishment, fair play, abuse of position, legal vs. moral, truth vs. lies, and right vs. wrong. Issues of a spiritual and moral nature meld with issues of law and public policy. Where do we draw appropriate lines? What is the role of personal morality in political life? Of course, it is perfectly necessary that we ask such questions and search for answers, but it is our imperfect, constantly failing humanity that causes us to do so. Would that Plato's or Christ's ideal teachings were the norm rather than dim and distant aspirations.

Looking in the strictly personal sphere, I examine my actions and the result of my actions. I find that almost without fail I receive the reward for doing right, the penalty for doing wrong. The reward may not be something tangible, such as money or a pat on the back; in fact, most often it is no such thing, rather an inner prompting from a Higher Power (the Holy Spirit?) that makes me *know* that I am on the right track. Similarly, punishment is more often than not an internal matter. Sure, I may have to pay a parking ticket or suffer a dressing-down from my spouse for a stupid indiscretion or misstep, but these overt corrections generally deal with surface issues that pop up on occasion—not the underlying causes of bad behavior.

If we assume that we are basically moral beings with good intentions who sometimes stumble on the path of life, rather than habitual criminals without a spiritual compass, we can still gain useful insight from Patrick's condemnation of the soldiers. He emphasized the steep cost of outrageous behavior—in this case slaughter, kidnapping, enslavement. There is no greater price to pay than to be bound to Satan as his slave for eternity. Those who fear God have nothing to fear from the forces of evil. Those who obey His law are blessed with peace of mind and an abundance of grace that helps one make it through the tedious ups and downs that otherwise try our spiritual mettle.

I dread not so much the apocalyptic finality of Judgment Day, though perhaps I should, as the everyday situations that draw out the worst in me: impatience with my children, intolerance of those with whom I disagree, anger at others for slights real and imagined, isolation from those who love me, procrastination about important responsibilities.

What brings me into disharmony with God and my fellow man? Conversely, what causes that marvelous experience of harmony and serenity? So much depends on my actions and reactions, minute by minute, day by day. How great is the payoff for taking that next right action! How painful is the emotional hangover after acting badly toward someone else.

If I can become (or remain) teachable, then I am surely redeemable in the eyes of my God. If I turn my eyes in His direction, I will make proper choices and live a life of love and service. My God metes out justice in a most loving way. It behooves me to stand before Him nakedly and honestly and accept His will for me. I have faith, based on experience, that injustice is never dealt from Him, only justice.

Prayer

Who am I to judge another? God, I ask that you give me clear sight to see myself—my motives, my thoughts, my actions, my omissions—in the light of my place among other human beings in this imperfect world. I should be harder on myself than anyone else, and with Your help I will be. Lord, make me an instrument of Your justice, that I may always look for the best in others and see the truth in their actions, as well as my own. Receive my prayer.

VOCATION

et again, many years later, I was taken captive. So on that first night I stayed with them. I heard a divine message saying to me: "You will be with them for two months more." And it happened that on the sixtieth night after that vision, the Lord delivered me from their hands. . . .

And again after a few years I returned to Britain to be with my kinfolk, who received me as their long-lost son and pleaded with me that now at last, having suffered such difficulties, I should promise them not to go away again.

And there one night I saw a vision of a man, whose name was Victoricus, coming it seemed from Ireland, with countless letters. He gave me one of them, and I read the first words of the letter, which were: "The Voice of the Irish." And as I read aloud the beginning of the letter I imagined that at the same moment I heard their voices—they were those very people who lived hard by the Wood of Foclut, which lies near the Western Sea [where the sun sets]—and thus did they cry out as one: "We ask you, holy boy, come back and walk among us once more."

I was quite brokenhearted and could read no more, and so I woke up. Thanks be to God, after many years the Lord granted to them their desire according to their prayer.

And on another night—whether within me or beside me, I know not, only God knows—they [the Irish] called out to me most unmistakably with words that I heard but could not quite understand, except that at the end of the prayer He spoke thus: "He who has laid down His own life for you, it is He who speaks to you." And so I awoke full of joy!

[*Confession*, ch. 21, 23–24]

Commentary

There can be no doubt of Patrick's utter commitment—physically, mentally, spiritually—to his vocation as priest, bishop, and apostle to the Irish Christian community. More, perhaps, than any of us alive today, he lived in an absolute certainty of purpose; he was crystal clear and unequivocal about his mission. Still, he lived with the knowledge of his apostleship for perhaps two decades or more before the Church actually called him to service; Patrick had been ordained a deacon and a priest only after years of study and preparation. Remember, he presumably had a lot of catching up to do academically and theologically. If we can take him at his word about his lack of proper education—and scholars believe we can—he was woefully unprepared, after the time of his captivity, for formal studies; whether through the accident of captivity, his own disinclination toward reading and writing, some unacknowledged disability, or simply by divine intention (or, perhaps, due to all of these reasons), Patrick's secular education ceased for several years, and he never mastered the basic rhetorical skills of his peers in the British clergy.

He also believed he was serving at the "end time," when Christ would soon return for the day of judgment. Patrick had been sent by God to the farthest land on earth, to the edge of the Western Sea, to bring the gospel message to men and women who, with very few exceptions (because there were some Christians in Ireland before Patrick arrived), had not yet received the opportunity for salvation. It was no easy task, and Patrick knew it. One can assume that very few British clergymen of the middle fifth century C.E. were itching to embark upon the quest that Patrick sought. After all, hostility between the Scots (that is, the Irish) and the Romanized Britons had not ceased. There were men like Coroticus (perhaps the father of the warlord Patrick would later excommunicate for atrocities against newly baptized Irish Christians) on the loose, as well as lesser warlords and bandits. Patrick knew the Irish people; he had been a slave among them. Despite this, he loved them and spoke their language, and so returned voluntarily to be among them.

And like St. Paul before him, Patrick's apostleship was revealed directly, received with alacrity, and executed with every ounce of energy the man could summon.

Patrick is called to his vocation by visions and voices. This theme runs throughout the *Confession*. He saw a vision of Victoricus, who carried letters from the Irish. Then he heard voices purported to be Irish who lived near the Western Sea. Then, another night, he heard them again.

One of the most moving moments in the *Confession* is

the next passage: "I imagined that at the same moment I heard their voices—they were those very people who lived hard by the Wood of Foclut, which lies near the Western Sea—and thus did they cry out as one: 'We ask you, holy boy, come back and walk among us once more.'"

Patrick himself was moved, "quite brokenhearted."

Who were these voices who called to Patrick in the night of his dreams?

Patrick was a bona fide mystic, but it is not very often that one makes a useful career of that talent. Instead, his calling was to put his mysticism—his faith in the voice of God as spoken through messengers sent directly to him—to work in the world among the Irish Christians. With both feet planted firmly on the earth, his heart and mind soared to the heavens; like prophets from Moses to Martin Luther King, Jr., Patrick was a corruptible man of the flesh who strove to live for a higher purpose. Sometimes he may not have understood exactly what God's purpose for him was; sometimes he may have obtained that deep, intuitive knowledge, and been as certain as any human being can be. It can be said that Patrick followed the rough, mysterious course laid out for him by God, and did it without complaint.

"And so I awoke full of joy!"

Even without knowing—as none of us know—what lay ahead on his soul-mission, Patrick accepted the job with enthusiasm.

Contemplation

What more important choice do we face than to decide what our life's work is going to be? Some know from childhood exactly what they will be "when they grow up." Others (like myself) might stumble onto a career path in our young adulthood that seems more or less to have been the right one. Some change careers radically in later life, even after retirement from a long-held job.

Vocation, however, is not just work and career. Vocation is a spiritual value that underlies one's work life. It is an idea that is perhaps a bit old-fashioned: like the concept of grace—God's blessing in my life—the concept of vocation is a direct benefit from Him that touches many aspects of our existence. Vocation implies that our eyes are turned toward God during hours of labor as well as hours of rest. He is ever present, and we must not lose sight of him even when we are "busy" earning a living.

Patrick knew where he was going; it had been revealed to him, even if his fellow clerics did not all agree with the course that he knew had been laid out. He clung to the vision of his apostolate to the Irish against all human opposition because he was convinced of the rightness of it, of its origin with the mind of God. Thus, with a clear goal, he directed his work to achieve that end: the Christianizing of the Irish people. There is no more straightforward definition of his vocation possible.

Where does that leave me, then? How do I know for certain what God's plan is for me? Am I doing the right thing today to conform to His will? Is my work life contributing to my spiritual growth, and do I have a positive influence on others in that realm of my life?

To ask the question is to answer it. I think that is what God expects: for us to examine our actions, our motives, the results. When I look back on my own situation, there have been too many uncanny threads, lucky breaks, coincidences of timing to get me to this point. If I had planned the result—which I did not—I could not have executed it as flawlessly as it has been wrought by my Creator. Certainly, I believe in luck and chance, but in the grander scheme of things, I know that I am being taken care of by the Father, and that if I stumble or make a wrong turn, I am not doomed to misery and failure. I may at some point be brought to a very different place—a not-so-comfortable place. But I can prepare myself for such a change through prayer and compassionate action.

A word about the substance of work: as the saying goes, God is found in the details. I often get bogged down in the minutiae of my responsibilities and feel overwhelmed by them. I become fearful of making a mistake or appearing incompetent. I procrastinate about certain tasks that eventually loom ever larger, growing out of proportion to their original size. I turn inward, become self-concerned, self-centered. There is only one way to break out of this pattern, and that is to seek God's help to handle one thing at a time, to do what is immediately in front of me. I must remember that there is a high level of personal satisfaction to be gained by a job well done—not to impress or to best another individual, but a job completed as well as I am capable of doing it.

My work and career afford me ways to be a productive member of the society of my fellows, by the grace of God. Each of us is called, in a way very similar to St. Patrick, to be the best possible person—to be of maximum service to God. In our own ways, large and small, public and private, we accomplish this mission. *This* is the meaning of vocation.

Prayer

What will you have me do, O Lord? I would follow Your will for my life. I ask for knowledge of Your will, for strength to accept Your will, for power to carry out Your will. More than just a career, a vocation is a means of service to You and to my family, friends, spiritual community. Please guide me to my place in Your kingdom on earth, among my fellow servants. Let me awaken unto Your will that my life may be made worthy in Your eyes and the eyes of my fellows.

ACCEPTANCE

This is why, never wearied, I tirelessly give thanks to my God, who kept me faithful on the day I was so sorely tried, so that today I can confidently offer Him my soul as a living sacrifice—to Jesus Christ my Lord, who preserved [defended] me from all of my tribulations.

Thus I can say to Him, "Who am I, O Lord, and what have You called me to do, You who assisted me with Your divine power that now I always praise and magnify Your name among the Gentiles wherever I may be, and not only in good days but also in times of danger?" So whatever happens to me, good or evil, I must accept readily and always give thanks to God, who has taught me to believe in Him always without hesitation. He must have heard my prayer so that I, however unworthy I was, should be granted the ability to undertake this holy and wonderful challenge in these last days; in this way I imitate those who, as the Lord foretold long ago, would preach His Gospel as a message to all nations and tribes before the end of the world. So we *have seen it happen, and so the prediction has been fulfilled. We ourselves are witnesses that the Gospel has been carried unto those places beyond which no one lives.*

[*CONFESSION*, CH. 34]

Commentary

Paradoxically, the strong-willed man who was utterly convinced of his life's mission had to be willing to give it up, to let it go, at a moment's notice. His is an example of how one can work and struggle and cling tenaciously to an idea, knowing that he does not control the outcome—that the results always lie in God's hands alone. Patrick knew the profound peace of mind that such acceptance can bring.

Throughout the *Confession* we are exposed to Patrick's ruthless honesty about himself. It is sometimes painful to read about his harsh experiences as a very young man, about the treatment he received from his peers in the British Church, about his lack of facility with language, about his times of temptation. Sometimes the document reads like a novel—and at other times, like a catechism. In trying to describe and defend his mission, the bishop relies heavily on scriptural quotations (primarily from the New Testament) that illustrate his themes. The Latin Bible was his constant guide, and he lived and breathed the book without apology.

From his Bible he learned the lesson of acceptance, especially in the example of Jesus, the Word made flesh who lived among sinners. It is startling, to me, to remember that St. Patrick lived a mere four hundred years after the time of Christ and within the same (or very similar, if dying) imperial system. Certainly four centuries was plenty of time for hearts to harden and the gospel message to become diluted, but Patrick sought to learn, to teach, and to live as closely to the Christ message as possible.

Like Christ, Patrick was tireless in his ministry, totally unselfish, believing that hard work in the vineyard of his Master was his ultimate and only purpose. "Patrick's mission almost seems a race against time; world events are getting worse, there is no time to be lost in carrying out the Lord's work." [Skinner, p. 24]

The place where he was put by God was, to him and to others in the late Roman world, the farthest point of human existence. The time in which he lived was thought to be the last phase of human life on earth before the second coming of the Redeemer. This worldview was not something strange or quaint—as it may appear to us today—but an accepted idea upon which Patrick's theology was based. After all, out at the ragged edges of the Roman empire where Patrick had grown up, there was a sense of impending chaos, if not a very real experience of it. What must have been Patrick's reaction upon hearing of the depredations of Coroticus against fellow converts newly christened by the bishop himself? Surely, this outrage was one of the prophesied indications of the impending fate of all mankind.

Patrick did not have to undergo any mental transformation to accept the "fact" of the "end times," any more than we have to struggle to accept the fact of television or computer technology or space travel. Impending perdition was simply a thread in the fabric of St. Patrick's fifth-century world, fueling his passion and sense of urgency.

Throughout his writings, Bishop Patrick emphasizes his utter trust in God. He is willing to expose his own shortcomings to other men, not without fear of their judgment but with the ultimate faith that their low opinion of him is less important than God's unconditional, undying love. He is willing to venture beyond which no Christian has ever traveled to take the gospel message to the "Gentiles" in a forbidding, foreign land of untold dangers and deeply ingrained opposition. He is willing to confront the warlord Coroticus at probable risk of his own life and perhaps others'—if the leader chooses to seek vengeance upon further innocents. Patrick is, in other words, out on a limb with little tangible means of support. Yet there is a blitheness and even happiness in his fulsome descriptions of these situations, because underlying all is God—his constant strength.

Given this total investment of himself in his spiritual Father, Patrick's example of acceptance is compelling. He was not one to go halfway. He was an all-or-nothing kind of guy. And those around him must have felt his powerful aura of faith and been impressed (or put off) by it. Thus as he walked the beautiful and treacherous terrain of Ireland he cared less about his personal fate than about the souls of those who needed, in his estimation, to hear the gospel message. And Patrick knew that if he put one foot in front of another in this task, God would ensure the results.

Having experienced the Creator's mercy and forgiveness at every stage of his long life, having survived dangers and difficulties without number (beyond the "twelve dangers" he mentioned in the *Confession*), having been enslaved and slapped down and pushed aside and betrayed, having seen the results of his strenuous work in the conversion of many thousands, having witnessed the rapid growth of the Church in Ireland, Patrick might look back with some self-satisfaction; he did not. Instead, he was satisfied that God had shown to the people His power and presence. Patrick was the medium, in this case, and he did not take any credit.

Without sitting still for a moment, he accepted his place in the eternal scheme; he accepted the love of his Father in heaven; he accepted the myriad faults in his own makeup; he accepted the obstacles placed in his path. Seeking ever and always to do God's will, St. Patrick made his life one of the most powerful examples of acceptance that can be found in the annals of Christianity.

Contemplation

The practical solution to many of my problems and mistakes is to accept the past and continue to work, in the present, to improve my character. As with all spiritual work, I do not have to labor in silence or alone: God is always available to me if I ask for His aid.

First, like Patrick, I must strip myself down to a virtual spiritual nakedness and stand before Him with no pretense, no hidden agenda, no corrupt motive; there is room only for total honesty between me and my Maker. I can then take a candid look at my present condition. What are my expectations of God? of myself? of my spouse and family members? of friends and colleagues? of people I encounter in daily life? of public figures and leaders? How realistic are these expectations?

Especially when I ask the question of myself, I know that I—like most people—am harder on myself than on anyone else. This is how Patrick also appears to me in his succinct and honest self-appraisal; he battled with his own expectations for many years, until he came to a place where he could look back at the fruitlessness of such effort. So what causes me not to accept present circumstances? Am I dissatisfied with aspects of my physical being, my health, my appearance, even my very mortality? Is my house big enough to measure up to my ego? Is my job not prestigious or lucrative enough to satisfy me? What is the quality of my faith, my religious life, my position within the parish? Do I have any reason to be unhappy with my lot? Examining these and other questions, I can answer—with as much honesty and objectivity as possible—that I have no reason to be unhappy or dissatisfied, either with the external condition or with my interior life.

This does not mean that all is problem-free. Bills must be paid. I must show up at work in order to qualify for a paycheck. A regular workout and fewer cheeseburgers would go a long way toward a slimmer, trimmer me. A more cooperative, relaxed, and understanding attitude at home might considerably ease tensions within the family. I can be of service to my children and my parish and my God without title or pretense, simply by showing up.

I believe that self-acceptance, then, is the first step in the process to total acceptance of others and, most importantly, of God's will for me. I can follow this step with the attempt to practice acceptance in every other aspect of my life and with every person I deal with. This is probably the most difficult but most rewarding task; for, if I can cease looking at life as a battle to be won—over foes real and imagined—then I go a long way toward total trust in God. After all, do I have to win every argument with my wife and children? Must I struggle with every driver who has the temerity to pass me on the highway? Must I question every directive that comes from my boss because it might make me uncomfortable or cause me to work harder than I'd care to? Must I succumb to anger at statements from political leaders with whom I disagree? To what degree do I have any personal power over the people and situations in the world at large?

The answer to these and other questions is: God has the power. I do not. I can govern my own actions and thoughts, to a great degree. I can improve the quality of my behavior and thinking, no doubt. Also, I can pray for the ability to live in the world with less friction and less anxiety. I can mind my own business and give credit to others when it is the right thing to do. God has the power to calm my spirit in the face of disturbance and to spark the good in the soul of another. I am not God, He is.

How wonderful it is to throw in the towel, to surrender the battle, to put down the burden! This does not mean that we must sit back and "take it," or do nothing to change circumstances or personal behaviors that are harmful to ourselves and others. But acceptance does mean that I can let go and let God infuse my life with his healing grace. When I put Him back in control (that is, accept the fact that He is already in control!), I instantly feel better, more at peace, calmer of mind and spirit. How simple it is! It allows me the freedom to live and breathe more easily.

Once a human being, always a human being. There is only one God, and He is available to us if we put aside the self-created obstacles to His presence. Perhaps I will try this path today and accept Him fully and completely, without reservations, in my life.

Prayer

As we often say in the Serenity Prayer: God, grant me the serenity to accept the things I cannot change, courage to change the things I can, and wisdom to know the difference. I beg for the humility and honesty to be able to accept Your will for me; I beg for the open-mindedness to see that my way is not always the best way, that I do not know what God's plan is for me and for others—despite best intentions and good motives. Lord Jesus, teach me to seek acceptance of God's will in all things.

THE CHURCH

*Y*ou know, and God knows, too, that I have lived among you since my youth in true faith and with a sincere heart. I have kept faith, and will always keep faith, even with the heathen tribes among whom I live. God knows I have neither cheated nor been false to any of them, nor even thought of doing so, for fear that I would cause them to attack God and His Church, and to persecute all of us, and lest the name of the Lord be blasphemed because of me. For it is written: "Woe to the man through whom the name of the Lord is blasphemed."

But though I was untaught in many skills, yet I have done all that I could to protect myself in my dealings with the Christian brethren, with the virgins of Christ, and with the devout women who freely presented me with trinkets or tossed their valuable ornaments onto the altar [for me]. I returned all these gifts to them again, though they were offended because they did not understand my reasons. I acted as I did because of my hope *for immortality. By being cautious in all my affairs, unbelievers could not criticize me or tarnish the Church, and I would not, even in the smallest detail, give anyone pretext to discredit or defame my ministry.*

Is it possible, then, that in the baptizing of so many thousands of people, I received or wished to receive even half a coin [scriptula, or scruple] from anyone? Just tell me and I shall repay it to the giver! Or when the Lord, through my very mediocre talents, ordained clergy far and wide, and I conferred His ministry to all without charge—if I asked any of them for so much as the price of a shoe, speak out and I will return it.

Instead, it was I who spent on your behalf, so that they would receive me. I traveled among you and went everywhere, often at great personal peril, even to the remotest parts of the land beyond which there is nothing and nobody, where no one had ever come to baptize, to ordain priests, or to confirm the faithful. By the Lord's grace, I have done all this, conscientiously and gladly, for your salvation.

[*CONFESSION*, CH. 48–51]

Commentary

Although St. Patrick did not himself introduce Christianity to Ireland, and though he was not the first bishop sent to the existing Christian community there (Palladius briefly held that distinction in 431 C.E.), he can be properly credited with establishing the Church on Irish soil. Patrick drew together the scattered pockets of believers—most, possibly, captured Britons like himself—and converted others through his decades of ministry by the scores and hundreds, and he boldly created a structure (featuring monasteries, parishes, and the see of Armagh) that survived him to this very day. It is possible, even likely, that other men than Patrick might have built an enduring Church in Ireland, but would they have left such an indelible personal mark on the institution as the dynamic apostle did?

Recent historical and archaeological findings make clear that the Christian Church already had fairly deep roots in the British Isles by the late fourth and early fifth centuries. From Palestine to Hibernia—remembering that the Irish were outside the sphere of direct Roman political influence—Christianity spread inexorably, passed from individuals and small groups to others by personal witness.

Dáibhí Ó Cróinín, in *Early Medieval Ireland*, lays out quite lucidly a historical scenario of the development of the Church in Ireland, beginning with the ordination and mission of Palladius, who, according to the *Chronicle* of Prosper of Aquitaine, was appointed by Pope Celestine I to minister "to the Irish believing in Christ." Ó Cróinín explores the histories of the Church in Gaul and Britain (Patrick's home) and shows, not surprisingly, that they were mutually dependent upon each other for the preservation and teaching of doctrine as well as the formation of clergy. Ó Cróinín makes a rather stark statement that puts Patrick and the situation he faced in a unique context: "It is important to remember that the early church, after St. Paul, had no concept of mission; it made no organized or official approach to non-believers; conversion was a matter for the individual. There is ample evidence to show that the post-Apostolic church developed no conscious institutionalized missionary effort or personnel; Christian teachers moved only among the converted, from one Christian household to the next." [Ó Cróinín, p. 18] Patrick, then, with his bold methods of proselytizing, shattered the mold.

Was the British Church strong enough and rich enough

to support a new diocese in forbidding Ireland? How much control, if any, did the Church of Rome wield in the decision to send a successor to Palladius—and who that successor would be? Was Patrick in fact the immediate successor to the man from Gaul? These are more questions that cannot be answered with authority, although scholars can guess confidently that the mother Church of the British Isles was solidifying its hold on the native Celtic populations with the same inevitability as the local church organizations elsewhere in Europe. It would still take at least four or five centuries, after Patrick, for the druidic and other indigenous cults of Ireland to die out almost completely.

The now-arcane yet fascinating debates fostered in the last century among Anglican and Catholic clergymen of the British Isles about Patrick's provenance and ordination illustrate how important and how mysterious a figure he became—and how both Protestants and Catholics wanted to claim him as their own. Dr. Todd's argument that St. Patrick was a neo-Protestant is supported in part by the conclusion that it was the British Church hierarchy—completely independent of Rome—who launched him on his historic mission. Most traditional accounts of Patrick's life, up to the mid-nineteenth century, assumed that his was a Roman appointment. Of course, there was more than a little politics involved in these opposing positions. The "two Patricks" debate flowed from the same stream of controversy and put scholars on notice that no assumptions about the saint would remain unchallenged—nor ought they to be.

It is now safely accepted that Patrick was a product of the British Church, who eventually sought to criticize and even sanction him, hence the defense presented in the *Confession*. At this very early stage in Christian history, St. Patrick established the foundation for a Church that would eventually look beyond Britain to Rome for validation. Pope John Paul II's position, as expressed to his audience of seminarians in 1979, reaches back to traditional sources to cement the connection with Rome; it might be interesting to explore one day whether the case for Patrick's appointment by Rome could be resurrected.

"We have no satisfactory way of knowing when Christianity became respectable; we only know that in Patrick's time it clearly still was not." We might say that Patrick himself was not "respectable," whether he clashed with his own superiors or the Irish aristocracy, he bucked the established power structures and confronted those in high places with his message of salvation. We learn in legendary accounts that the kings did not like him or his message. But when he was able to win over those in high places he made his ultimate task simpler: through this method of confrontation and conversion among the highborn, he sought to bring the gospel to common folks, as well.

This subject of how Patrick and his successors infused the Irish people with a love of the gospel makes for some of the most fascinating reading (Cahill, for example) of all. It is one of the greatest success stories of all time. And it is the most tangible, immediate legacy of the Apostle of Ireland.

Contemplation

The Church is my home, and my home is the Church. I write these words with surest conviction and deepest ambiguity. For any of us, I think, home is not only "where the heart is" but where conflicts and fears and sorrows arise. Who affects us more directly and deeply than members of our own household? Whom do we love and fight with and resent and need the most, if not our family? And where is this most private and intense emotional comedy-drama played out every day? At home.

A religious community and faith tradition (e.g., church, temple, mosque) is not a static or entropic entity—as it may sometimes appear. Rather, it will be as dynamic or as boring as I choose to make it for myself. Yes, I have a choice: whether and how much to participate in the life of the community. If I put something in, I may be able to take something out. So much is up to me.

Am I forgiving and tolerant of social slights and offenses by my fellow parishioners? Might they have problems they want to share if only someone would ask? Do I put out my hand to newcomers—and old-timers who may be taken for granted? Do I discuss with my family matters of faith and encourage them also to participate in the activities of our church, as well as the liturgy? Do I seek spiritual guidance from my pastor, who is the representative of the bishop and of Christ in our local community?

The church building itself attracts and enfolds the communicant. It is a temple and a spiritual headquarters. It is a gathering place for the faithful. The physical church represents the universal Church and the Body of Christ. When I stand with my family and my fellow parishioners to hear the Word, whether in a humble chapel or the most magnificent cathedral, I feel acutely that I am in the presence of God. I am reminded by the structure—the windows, the crucifix, the tabernacle, the majestic pillars—of the beauty of the Creator's design as reflected in the experience and abilities of his own creatures. The church building is a refuge from a noisy, confusing, threatening world; in the early morning for mass or for a quiet few minutes of prayer, it is the place where I can feel comfort and gain energy for the tasks I face in daily life.

I am the Church, and the Church is me. Like Patrick, I am deeply flawed and unworthy. Why bother, I sometimes ask myself? Why try to be "good," to behave in the way I was shown by my parents and by the priests and sisters and lay teachers who attempted to lay the foundations of morality beneath my feet? Sometimes it seems that the entire world has careened away from the path of righteousness, that I am fighting an uphill battle to do the next right thing, to avoid the occasion of sin, to give to another person rather than to take. Then it is time for me to step out of my self-centeredness into the light of Christ; it is time for me to remember that I am a member of a greater community of belief and action. I am the Church when I act in the manner that Christ taught. The Church is me when a dollar in the collection basket or a handshake or a prayer reaches another human being in need.

Jesus and the apostles, Patrick and the saints, the clergy and the laity of my parish, my family and myself: we are the Church.

Prayer

Bring me home, Father, into Your enfolding arms. I am the prodigal who wandered from Your love and sought to live according to the ways of the world. I seek to come back to Your love, to follow the way of Your Son. Open my ears and my mind and my heart to His message of salvation. Forgive me my sins and make me worthy to be counted one of Your people. I seek to be at home in this world among the community of believers.

COURAGE

*A*nd when I was attacked by certain of my elders, who came forward and brought up my sins against [as a challenge to] my hard-won episcopate, I was truly on that day so cast down that I might have fallen, now and for all eternity. But the Lord spared His disciple, who has chosen exile for His name's sake, and He came strongly to my aid during this time of humiliation. And since I did not fall badly into disgrace and reproach, and no harm came to me, I pray to God that it will not be reckoned against them [who brought these charges] as a sin.

After the lapse of thirty years they [these Churchmen] found a charge against me, raising the words of a confession that I had made just before I was ordained a deacon. When in a state of worry and sadness, I had privately confided to my dearest friend a sin I had committed one day in my youth—in fact, in a single hour of weakness. I cannot say for certain—though God surely knows—if I had yet reached the age of fifteen, and I was still, as I had been since my childhood, not a believer in the living God. But I remained in a state of death and unbelief until I was severely punished by the daily humiliations of hunger and nakedness.

Yet, while it was not of my own choice that I traveled to Ireland at the time when I was nearly a lost soul, it was well for me, because I was reformed [corrected] by the Lord, and He made me fit to be today what was once so unlikely and far removed from me: that I, who scarcely thought of my own salvation, should work for and tend to the salvation of others. . . .

Therefore, I give thanks to Him, who gave me strength in all things, not hindering me from the journey on which I had resolved, or from the difficult task that I had learned from Christ my Lord. Rather, I felt even more His limitless power [and virtue] within me; and my faith was approved before God and men.

I say boldly that my conscience does not bother me, neither now nor will it in the future, for I have God as my witness that I have not lied in all I have said to you.

[Confession, ch. 26–28, 30–31]

Commentary

Patrick's courage was epic in its proportion. It is difficult for us, at a remove of fifteen hundred years, to know of all the trials and physical dangers he faced, but we have several clues from his writings. He was no stranger to adventure, and his life was at risk many times: he was captured by Irish raiders, held as a slave, escaped on a perilous voyage, and endured deprivation and threats to his person. And somehow, at some point, Patrick found his way home to Britain.

Later, his life's purpose was threatened by colleagues

in the British Church. They stood directly in his path to appointment as bishop. In this case, he stood up to accusations that might have destroyed a lesser man.

When he wrote the *Confession*, St. Patrick was an elderly man at the end of his prodigious career as missionary bishop. The document was composed as a defense against unspecified (within the document itself) charges that had been lodged in Britain, challenging the old man's authority and competence. There is no independent record of the substance of these charges; we can infer their meaning only from Patrick's own words. His account is, prima facie, biased—yet as we have seen in this study of his nature, he was generally very hard on himself, perhaps preemptively self-critical.

Even a cursory examination of ancient Church history reveals a pattern of heresies and infighting and personal antagonisms that kept this very human institution roiling for centuries. Today it is still this way: controversies, scandals, sectarianism, competition, jealousies, doctrinal disputes. In Patrick's case, the accusations, both early and later, were personal. They were leveled to prevent him from winning an appointment in the first case and stripping him of his powers and authority in the second. Many times in his life, Patrick relates, he was brought low, *reprobatus sum*, rejected by all. Yet always he attempted to keep his eyes gazing upward to God. Let's look at the first instance in the context of Patrick's ability to stand up courageously to attack.

Patrick's courage was a deep spiritual resource; he drew on this resource to change and improve himself rather than to confront his opponents and force them to yield. The war he waged was primarily an internal one. His demons and enemies were the very shortcomings that he reveals in the *Confession* and the *Letter*: pride, ambition, righteousness.

Although he ultimately won his battles against his moral defects, it took tremendous sustained effort to do so. This is the manifestation of his courage.

Of course, external conditions affected him, as such conditions affect all of us. His enemies rose against him unexpectedly in the no doubt arcane and closed process of episcopal appointments. He had been assured by his best friend that the job was his. What a doubly devastating blow, then, to learn that not only would he be denied the bishopric, but that his friend had betrayed him, dashing his fondest hopes. Patrick was exposed and brought low, humiliated and chastised. Somehow he survived. No doubt he threw himself into prayer, study, and work.

He had to face the people who snatched the appointment from his grasp. Did they laugh at him? Did they scorn him? Did they ostracize him? Whatever they did, we know that *he* hung tough and eventually won the war. He was single-minded in his devotion to God and was convinced that somehow—if not now, then one day—he would be sent to the Irish.

When he received the appointment after the mission of Palladius ended prematurely (perhaps as early as 432 C.E., according to the Bury chronology), Patrick was steeled to the task; he had, we surmise, forgiven his enemies within the Church hierarchy, or at least put their destructive actions behind him. He rose from his earlier defeat, but there is no evidence that he did so at the expense of another. That was not his way.

In the course of his evangelization of Ireland, St. Patrick encountered constant threats to his life, as does any missionary in an alien land. We can only imagine the array of dangers that he would face in the course of his mission: harsh weather, hostile tribesmen, shortage of food, lack of

armed protection, threat of assassination, treacherous land-
scapes, political opposition from the emerging aristocracy,
and religious opposition from native druid cultists. In fact,
later in the *Confession*, he says that a "merciful and caring
God often freed me from slavery and from twelve dangers
that threatened my life—not to mention numerous traps
and plots," giving his readers a vivid, quantified sense of
these dangers. [ch. 35]

Seemingly, he met these challenges head-on, assuming
them to be part and parcel of the experience. He lived, after
all, in a time and place that had not felt the civilizing, if op-
pressive, presence of the Roman empire; the Romans had
not even attempted to invade the distant, dangerous island
of Hibernia, populated by fierce, undisciplined warriors.
He lived in a place not totally unfamiliar to him, having
spent six years of his life there, but each step he took as the
consecrated bishop of the Christian Irish brought him to
new places where he encountered new people and new
challenges to his message.

The legendary lives of Patrick are rife with duels and
violent confrontations, which may have been based, to
some degree, on the facts of his experience. Particularly,
these stories pit the saint against the so-called High King of
the Irish, Laoghaire, and weave a tapestry of troubles between the two of them. One interpretation of the hymn
called the Lorica, or the Deer's Cry, attributes to Patrick the
miraculous ability to change himself and his followers into
deer to escape the king's men who pursued them into the
forest to slay them. This tale is emblematic of the real dangers Patrick must have lived with virtually every day of his
ministry. And it reveals that his faith gave him courage, as
well as the power to survive.

Other legends highlight Patrick's steadfastness and

stubborn refusal to be deterred by obstacles of any type; always he is portrayed, rightly or wrongly, as the hero of the moment, the empowered apostle and miracle worker who was able to extricate himself and his followers from peril. But behind the legends and beneath the words of the *Confession* and the *Letter*, we gain a distinct sense of a man who was tempered by years of unrelenting challenge that he accepted as a necessary aspect of a life dedicated to Christ.

If courage is "grace under pressure," if it is fearlessness in the face of danger, if it is the ability to acknowledge one's fears, admit one's faults, and commit to changing oneself for the better—if courage is any or all of these things, St. Patrick possessed it and lived it on a grand scale.

Contemplation

In our day-to-day existence we may face threats to our livelihood, personal setbacks and disappointments, sometimes humiliations within the community of neighbors or peers. We may face threats to our life or physical well-being, or threats against those we love. We may know internal pressures that cause dark thoughts and feelings, which seem to overwhelm our ability to cope with reality. Rarely is life a problem-free romp in the playground.

I have choices about how to handle such situations. I can turn and run, deny the problem, isolate or hide. From Patrick's example I can learn instead how to face these challenges with a faith-based courage. Central to the saint's experience—and his response to particular situations—is the notion that God is a friend and protector who will not abandon the individual in need. For us, this is a powerful lesson, if only we will apply it to our own lives.

Courage is not the opposite of fear. We all live with

fear, deal with it day in and day out in virtually every aspect of our lives. American political scientist Hannah Arendt has written that fear is an emotion indispensable for survival, deeply ingrained in the human experience from the earliest days. Courage is the ability to accept fear and turn fear into an asset; courage operates hand in hand with faith. God would not bring me this far in the journey to drop me into the abyss, to abandon me to my enemies (real and imagined).

Courage is a lightener of the spirit. What an existence is promised us when we are freed from fears and resentments against others, when we speak the truth with no thought as to the consequences, when we accept just criticism as well as praise, when we do not care what others think of us—only what God thinks and what His will means for us. Courage allows us to fly, to soar toward our dreams, to live above the humdrum and commonplace.

Courage is a companion. Really, courage means that not only has God not abandoned me, but I have not abandoned God. It signifies an equal partnership. Patrick wrote: "Therefore, I give thanks to Him, who gave me strength in all things, not hindering me from the journey on which I had resolved, or from the difficult task I had learned from Christ my Lord. Rather, I felt even more His limitless power [and virtue] within me; and my faith was approved before God and men." [*Confession*, ch. 30]

The lesson is simple—but too often the student is unable or unwilling to hear the teacher. Why should I remain fearful about losing my job, my health, my family, my bank account, the esteem of my friends, control of events (as if I ever had it in the first place), or about what another person thinks of me? The courage to trust God is all that I lack. It is so simple, and so profound.

Prayer

Today I pray for the courage to face the difficulties that all children of God must face. In my circumstance, I believe that I will not be given more than I can handle; while any one problem or situation may seem overwhelming, I know that God is with me if I set myself in concert with His will. I pray for the courage to act in accordance with God's will, no matter the opposition or the cost of such action. For if it is right, it is of God, and He will be my support and comfort. He is the giver of courage to the fearful.

GRATITUDE

*T*his is why, never wearied, I tirelessly give thanks to my God, who kept me faithful on the day I was so sorely tried, so that today I can confidently offer Him my soul as a living sacrifice—to Jesus Christ my Lord, who preserved [defended] me from all of my tribulations.

Thus I can say to Him, "Who am I, O Lord, and what have You called me to do, You who assisted me with Your divine power that now I always praise and magnify Your name among the Gentiles wherever I may be, and not only in good days but also in times of danger?" So whatever happens to me, good or evil, I must accept readily and always give thanks to God, who has taught me to believe in Him always without hesitation. He must have heard my prayer so that I, however unworthy I was, should be granted the ability to undertake this holy and wonderful challenge in these last days; in this way I imitate those who, as the Lord foretold long ago, would preach His gospel as a message to all nations and tribes before the end of the world. So we have

seen it happen, and so the prediction has been fulfilled. We ourselves are witnesses that the gospel has been carried unto those
places beyond which no one lives.

I am very deeply in God's debt, He who gave me such grace
that so many people were reborn in God through me and afterward confirmed in the Church, and that priests were ordained
for them everywhere, for a people just awakening to faith. They
are the Lord's chosen, from the outermost parts of the earth, as
He had previously promised through His prophets: "The Gentiles
shall come to You from the far ends of the earth, and they shall
say, 'How false are the idols that our fathers made for themselves, and there is no use in them.'" And again: "I have set You
as a light among the heathen nations, so that You may be the
way to salvation even as far as the utmost part of the earth."

[*Confession*, ch. 34, 38, 59]

Commentary

At this point in his *Confession*, Patrick takes stock of his
situation and reaches some conclusions. He looks back at
all the souls he has saved and all the good he has done; although he does not minimize his accomplishments as
apostle to the Irish, nor dismiss the many thousands he has
brought to Christ, he knows that whatever he has achieved
has not been due to his talents and efforts. He was the instrument of God's will. So he reiterates his personal unworthiness and shortcomings.

As we have seen, Patrick was no stranger to peril. What
is fascinating is that, even at this late date (as he composed
the *Confession*, he was an old man), he expects to be the victim of assassination or treachery. He expects no congratula-
tions for his accomplishments from his Church for he

knows that he is tainted, damaged goods, that those who do not ridicule him for forsaking his station in Britain to spend time shepherding the Irish consider him unworthy for that. Yet all Patrick can do is fulfill his role as the instrument of the divine will and fill out the mission of the saintly—that of bringing the word of God to the farthest reaches of the earth. He does not seek thanks or rewards for his job well done; his concern is to find a way he can express his gratitude for the privilege of leading this perilous existence.

For two centuries after the *Confession* (that is, well into the seventh century C.E.), the name of Patrick was not mentioned in Christian documents, and he was not a figure about whom legends were composed for some centuries more; that is one primary reason that there are so many inconsistencies and anachronisms in the legends. Yet, in the monasteries of Ireland, *someone* preserved and copied the *Confession* and the *Letter*, studied and recited them, cherished them, preserved them for future generations until a time the Church would find the invocation of his name useful. I am sure that the monks understood that Patrick, in his own words, is tireless; he will tell all who will listen; he will not stop preaching about God's light and his own gratitude. He takes up the ultimate challenge known to man: to imitate Christ and live the gospel message. In so doing, he makes himself an example, an ideal that later generations might do well to imitate.

He accepts the position of debtor to his heavenly Father, acknowledging his place in the long Biblical line of prophets and apostles, accepting this position as neither more nor less than it is. He puts on his cloak, perhaps a few rude symbols of his episcopal office, and goes out among the people. And he is ever grateful.

Contemplation

How do we express our gratitude? How do we give thanks? Patrick's answer is: by giving everything we have and claiming nothing for ourselves. There cannot come a time when we have "nothing left to give," because then we cease to be and we are no more. When we regard our lives as fonts of love, of mercy, of charity, there can be no alternative.

But who are we talking about? What sort of a person can make a commitment like this, honestly? And fulfill it most of the time, in the hectic busyness of our modern lives? The truth is, I rarely have the time or tranquillity to think about these matters with any seriousness or dedication. The world crowds in more and more, faster and faster, and it is rare that I am aware of anything but the din of living.

So I read Patrick's self-appraisal with astonished wonder, and with envy. What it must be like to be so committed! How gratifying it must be to be so loving of righteousness and godliness that the most longed-for end is to be a martyr for the Lord's name. How fulfilling it must be to be so dedicated to giving, to saving, to helping, that no spiritual limit bars any sacrifice or charity, but that it is only the bonds of the flesh that hold one back.

I can only wonder what it would be like to operate on that plane.

Gratitude, for me, is a practical and powerful resource. It is a key that unlocks the door to peace of mind. It is a lever that lifts burdens from one's shoulder. Simply by thanking God for what He has given me—rather than dwelling on what I want and don't have—I receive a remarkable uplift, a relief from mundane cares. I am reminded of a prayer

I heard somewhere: "God, thank You for what You have given me; thank You for what You have taken from me; thank You for what You have left me."

Can it really be this simple? I believe it to be so. I believe that the Father does not give us more that we can handle, that He does not seek to complicate our lives; we do that ourselves. Instead, the Creator is profoundly simple in His being and in His message to us.

As Patrick and other writers put it, God is "a light among the nations." I am obligated to seek the divine light, that it may illuminate the world for me. Also, I am called to expose myself to His light; it warms me and guides me in the darkness, just as it sustained St. Patrick through many dark and difficult times. The light shows me who I am, allowing me to appraise my spiritual condition.

Working hand in hand with humility, gratitude is an attitude that requires candor: to see things for what they are, to want what I already have, to seek no advantage over another.

Prayer

My Lord, if I cannot see what is inside me, then I pray that You look, and turn me into a tool for good and a vessel of grace. If I have a selfless, giving nature, help me to see it, nurture it, use it to help others by doing Your will. And if I have nothing inside me but the sinews of need and desire that move the beasts of Your creation, let me be clay in the hands of the righteous and an instrument for the will of the holy. And if I can see who I am, let me, I pray, joyfully find a life I am ready to give to Your service.

A F T E R W O R D

In his introductory notes to his new translations of the *Letter* and the *Confession*, John Skinner re-creates a vivid image:

> One of the treasured relics said to have belonged to Patrick—if one might admit the slightest whiff of myth—is the reliquary case in which his mass bell was once kept. We can imagine Patrick rousing his flock with a clanking cowbell and inviting them to come to his morning Eucharist. The bell has long since disappeared, but more precious by far is the sound of his own words ringing across fifteen centuries. [Skinner, p. xxx]

What St. Patrick left behind, whether it was his intention or not, is a word-picture of his soul. Faded, like an old photograph, and frayed, like an ancient tapestry too often exposed to the elements, his testament reveals a passionate and charismatic man who, while certain unto death of his mission, had long since put his ultimate destiny into the hands of his Creator. After all, it was God who delivered him out of bondage—just as He had delivered the Israelites—and God who found him buried like a rough stone deep in the mire and lifted him out, "in His mercy," and raised him to "the very top of the wall" where he could see and be seen, hear and be heard.

Yes, we can hear the cry of this great soul echoing through the ages! I find it irresistible and feel that it calls to me somehow. Perhaps others will feel the same way: that they can learn from this teacher—this hunter and fisher of fellow souls—who sought only and ever to carry the message of salvation to the "Gentiles" at the very ends of the earth. Little did he realize that his zeal would triumph over time and space and human limitations.

Whenever I spoke to friends about this project I called it simply "a book about St. Patrick." Inevitably, the first response was, "What about those snakes? Did he really—?" No, he didn't, I told them. Then I began spilling out facts and lore about the man, eager to sketch in a few words about this complex figure. Inevitably, the second response was, "I didn't know that." Of course, neither had I until just several months prior, but I enjoyed sharing these bits of historical arcana. I learned quickly, however, not to say too much—for I did not want to spoil my precious discovery.

I wanted, at first, to hoard the spiritual wisdom of this saint. I enjoyed the solitary search for his words and his meanings. Many a Saturday morning I burrowed into the stacks at Walsh Library on the Seton Hall campus, away from the world of my everyday existence, alone but for the company of Patrick.

But he would not have it that way; he was a preacher, after all—a pastor who ministered to a large, needy flock.

There is such an urgency to his every word; he was not one to hold back. For him, it was all-out, all the time, because he believed there was very little time remaining to save the souls of the Irish.

Of course, none of us has much time—or "enough" time—to accomplish the soul work that our Creator has assigned to us. We, too, should feel Patrick's urgency, for in point of fact, these are our own "last days" at "the ends of the earth." I say this not to inject a note of gloom and doom, but to remind myself that, while one day it may be too late, it is never too early to get to work in the vineyard. I have been blessed with forty-plus years to make a beginning on a task that I know has no ending. Each day—"I arise today"—I have an opportunity to take a step forward, into the light. When I choose not to (and there are days when I make that choice) it is, in effect, a step backward. And it is all the more difficult to recover the lost opportunity.

Patrick calls me to take that step—today:

I arise today
    with God's strength to pilot my course,
    with God's power to uphold me,
    with God's wisdom to guide me,
    with God's eye to give me seeing,
    with God's ear for my hearing,
    with God's word for me to speak,
    with God's hand to guard me,
    with God's path to become my road,
    with God's shield to protect me,
    with God's army to insure my salvation:
        against every demon's trap,
        against the lure of sin,
        against lustful instincts,
        against those who wish me ill, far and near.

[TRANSLATION BY G.T.]

He teaches me that I do not have to accomplish this soul-building task all at once, nor all alone. In fact, I was not designed that way: my strength and hope comes from God. He is the Source of all that is good within me. He is the Potential that I seek within myself and others. He is the Higher Power that defeats the lower powers of pride and fear. He is the Word that fills my ear and my mind and my heart. St. Patrick reminds me of the majesty and the miracle of this gospel message of Christ.

I am very grateful that Patrick found me. Whether through fortunate accident or providential design, I am descended from the people to whom he was called to minister: "We ask you, holy boy, come back and walk among us once more." [*Confession*, ch. 23] The Voice of the Irish had reached him in his dream-vision, and he responded to them with every ounce of energy he possessed. To them—to God—he devoted his life. I came along a lot later—some fifteen hundred years later. Yet he found me. His appeals to the Scots warlord and the Christian clergy in his native Britain somehow were also addressed to me; in the particularity of his communications lay a universality that transcended time and language.

Will I, then, take up St. Patrick's challenge to follow the path trod by the Son, to breathe in the presence of the Holy Spirit, to worship and obey the Father? Do I have the courage to accept God's grace each day and live a more selfless life of gratitude and service? Perhaps. At least I have the inspiring testimony of a man who did all that and more in the time he spent among the ancient Irish.

I can hear that old mass bell sounding across the green fields of time. Can you?

A Note on the Translations

For the Patrician texts in this book I most often consulted five different English translations of the saint's Latin writings and drew from them as I composed my own interpretation of St. Patrick's surviving works. Underpinning all and informing my earliest readings of the *Confession* and the *Letter* is Ludwig Bieler's seminal version found in *The Works of St. Patrick* (pp. 21–47). All writers who have worked subsequent to Bieler owe him an incredible debt. For example, Paul Gallico's biography, *The Steadfast Man*, was the first major book-length biography of St. Patrick for a general audience that drew on Bieler's monumental achievement.

R.P.C. Hanson is another giant of Patrician scholarship and interpretation. *The Life and Writings of the Historical Saint Patrick* (pp. 58–125) contains the most helpful glosses on the meaning and intent of Patrick's sometimes confusing prose, as well as notes that direct the reader to relevant scriptural references from the Latin Bible.

Two extremely helpful translations are from *The Legacy of Saint Patrick* by Martin P. Harney, S.J. (pp. 93–129) and *Saint Patrick's World* by Liam de Paor (pp. 96–113). De Paor's especially renders the rustic Latin into sinewy, comprehensible contemporary English, and his book places the writings of the saint into a vivid context: these two documents, de Paor writes, "give us, not his exterior, but his interior, history."

Finally, and most recently, John Skinner has produced a lyrical translation in *The Confession of Saint Patrick* (pp. 1–76). Like the best English-language versions of classic epic poetry, the Skinner rendering is alive and flashing with personal insight; here Patrick is as much poet as preacher, without subsuming the sincerity of his faith in God.

My own version of the complete texts of St. Patrick's *Confession* and *Letter* follow.

Appendix A
The Confession of
St. Patrick

1. I am Patrick, a sinner, the most unlearned [i.e., rustic, unschooled] and least of all the faithful, and utterly despised by many. My father was a certain man named Calpornius, a deacon, son of the late Potitus, a presbyter, who was in the town of Bannaventa Berniae. He had a small estate nearby. There I was captured and made a slave. I was not even sixteen years old. I was ignorant of the true Lord, and so I was led to Ireland in captivity with many thousands of others, who deserved this fate, because we cut ourselves off from God, because we did not keep His commandments, because we were disobedient to our priests who admonished us about our salvation.

And so the Lord revealed to us His wrath and indignation and scattered us among many nations [heathen tribes], even unto the farthest ends of the earth, where I am now, in my lonely insignificance, among strangers.

2. Then the Lord opened my mind and senses to the

nature of my unbelief so that I may—however late—remember my sins and turn with all my heart to the Lord my God. He turned His attention to my abject humility [insignificance] and took pity on my youth and ignorance. He watched over me and protected me before I knew Him and before I was wise enough to distinguish between good and evil. He strengthened and comforted me as a father consoles a son.

3. Thus I cannot remain silent—nor would it be appropriate for me to do so—about the great benefits and graces that the Lord has granted me in the land of my captivity. For this is the repayment we make to God for what He revealed during our capture and enslavement: We must exalt and preach the wonders of God to all the races and nations that are under the heavens.

4. Because there is no other God, nor has there ever been, nor will there ever be, other than God the unbegotten Father, who is without beginning, from whom all has beginning, the Ruler of the universe, as we have been instructed; and His only Son Jesus Christ, whom we proclaim has always been together with the Father, and who was begotten spiritually by the Father in a way impossible to explain, before the beginning of the world, before all beginning; and by Him all things are made, visible and invisible.

Jesus was made man, and having triumphed over death was received into heaven by the Father; and the Father has given Him full power over all names in the heavens and on earth, and in hell, and every tongue shall confess to Him that Jesus Christ is Lord and God, in whom we believe, and whose second advent we expect very soon, judge of the living and of the dead who will return to every man according to what he has done. And He [God the Father] has poured out upon us so abundantly the Holy Spirit, the gift and pledge of immortality, who makes those who believe and obey become sons of God and equal inheritors with Christ. We confess and adore Him—one God in the Trinity of the Most Holy Name.

5. For He has Himself said through His prophet: "Call upon Me in the day of your trial and trouble, and I will rescue you; and you shall glorify Me." And He has said: "It is honorable to reveal and preach the works of God."

6. Even though I am imperfect in so many aspects of my life, nevertheless I wish that my brethren and my family should know what sort of person I am, so that they may clearly understand my heart and soul's desire [my mettle].

7. I know very well the testimony of my Lord, who in the psalm plainly teaches: "You will destroy those who speak lies." And again He declares: "The mouth that lies kills a man's soul." And the same Lord says in the Gospel: "Every idle word that people shall speak, they will be asked to account for it on the day of judgment."

8. So I cannot be unaware of these Gospel warnings. Indeed, I am filled with fear and trembling of such a sentence on that day, when no one will be able to escape or hide; but all of us, without exception, shall be called to own up to even our smallest sins before the tribunal of Our Lord Jesus Christ, the Son of the Father.

9. Because of this I have for a long time intended to write, but until now have hesitated; for I was afraid of exposing myself to the talk [criticism] of men, because I have not gotten a proper education like the others who thoroughly and easily absorbed both the law and the sacred Scripture, and never had to change from the language of their childhood. Instead, they were able to polish it and make it more perfect. Whereas in my case, what I write or speak must be translated into a tongue that is still foreign to

me; this can be easily proved from the flavor of my writing, which reveals how little instruction and training I have had in the art of rhetoric. As the Scripture says, "By his tongue [language] the wise man will be known—as will understanding and knowledge and truth."

10. But what help are excuses, however true, especially if combined with the presumption [audacity] of old age? I attempt to gain something at this stage that I did not achieve in my youth. At that time my own sins prevented me from understanding in my mind what I had previously just barely read. But who believes me now, even if I should reiterate what I have already said?

As a youth—that is, as a beardless boy unable to articulate my thoughts—I was taken captive before I knew what to pursue in my life and what to avoid. So today I blush and fear more than anything to reveal my lack of education. For I lack the skill to tell my story to those versed in the art of concise writing [learned men]—in such a way that my soul and mind long to do, and so that the sense of my words expresses what I really mean.

11. Indeed, if advantages had been given to me as they were to others, then I would not be silent, but I would be able to express my gratitude. Perhaps some people think me arrogant for doing so, in spite of my lack of learning and my slow tongue. After all, it is written: "The stammering tongues shall quickly learn to speak peace."

How much more should we earnestly strive to do this, we who are, so Scripture says, a letter of Christ for salvation even to the utmost ends of the earth, and though not an eloquent one, yet . . . written in your hearts not with ink, but with the spirit of the living God! And again the Spirit witnesses that even rusticity [backwardness] was made by the Most High Creator.

12. So therefore I, at once a rustic and an exile, unlearned, who does not know how to provide for the future—this at least I know with complete certainty that before I was humiliated I was like some big stone lying deep in the mud; and He who is all-powerful came and in His mercy lifted me up and raised me aloft to a place on the very top of the wall. Therefore I should cry out aloud and so also render something back to the Lord for His great benefits here and throughout eternity—gifts that the simple mind of man is unable to comprehend.

13. For this reason then, be astounded, all of you great and small who fear God, and you men of rhetoric on your estates, listen and pay attention to this. Who was it that raised me up, fool that I am, from among those who in the eyes of men are considered wise and expert in the law and powerful in speech and in everything? And He inspired me—me, a despised outcast of this world—above many others, to be the man (if only I could!) who, with reverence and without complaint, should faithfully serve the race of Gentiles to whom the love of Christ brought me and left me for the remainder of my life, if I should be so worthy; yes, to serve them humbly and sincerely.

14. Consequently, by the light of our rule of faith in the Holy Trinity, I must make this decision, disregarding any personal danger; I must make known the gifts of God and His everlasting solace. Boldly and without any fear I must faithfully preach everywhere the name of God, so that even after my own death I might leave a spiritual legacy to my brethren and my children whom I have baptized in the Lord—so many thousands of people.

15. And I was in no way worthy, nor was I the sort of person that the Lord would grant such a gift to me, His humblest servant: that after my many hardships and misfortunes, after such great difficulties and burdens, after my captivity and enslavement, after so many years living among the Irish, He should give me so great a grace in behalf of this nation of people—something that once, in my boyhood, I never dreamed nor could even hope for.

16. But after I was taken to Ireland [as a slave]—then every day I was forced to tend flocks of sheep in the pasture. As I did so, many, many times throughout the day I prayed. The love of God and the awe [fear] of Him grew strong within me more and more, and my faith was strengthened also. And my soul was restless within me so that in a single day I would say as many as a hundred prayers, and almost as many in the night, and this even when I was staying in the woods or on the mountainside. I often awakened and prayed before daylight—through snow, through frost, through rain—and I felt no illness or discomfort, and I was never lazy but filled with energy and inspiration. Now I know this was because the Holy Spirit was fervent [glowing] within me.

17. And there one night in my sleep I heard a voice saying to me: "It is good that you fast, for soon you will return to your own country." And once again, after a short time I heard the voice tell me: "Come see, your ship is ready." But it was not near. It lay at a distance of perhaps two hundred miles away, and I had never been there, nor did I know a living soul there. Soon after, I took to flight and left behind the man to whom I had been a bond servant for six years. And I traveled with the strength of God who directed my way successfully, and I feared nothing until I reached that ship.

18. And the very day that I arrived at the harbor the ship was setting to sea, and I said that I was able to pay for my passage with them. But the captain was angry, and he answered my request harshly: "It is of no use for you to ask us to go along with us!" When I heard this, I turned and left them to return to the hut where I was staying. And as I walked away, I began to pray; and before I had even ended my prayer I heard one of them shouting behind me, "Come, hurry, we shall take you onboard in good faith. Be our friend in your own way."

And so on that day I refused to suck their breasts [a customary appeal for friendship and protection] for fear of my God and their pagan ways, but still I hoped they would come to faith in Jesus Christ. And so I had my way with them and joined them, and we set sail immediately.

19. In three days we made landfall, and we journeyed for twenty-eight days through a deserted, barren wilderness. No food was to be found and hunger overcame them. One day the captain turned to me and said, "What do you say, Christian? You claim that your God is great and powerful. So why don't you pray for us? For we are in immediate danger of starving; we may not live to see another human being ever again." Then I said confidently [and calmly] to them: "Trust with all your hearts in the Lord my God—for Him nothing is impossible—so that this day He may send you enough food for your journey until you are satisfied. For He has abundance everywhere."

By the hand of God, so it came to pass. Suddenly, right before our eyes, a herd of swine appeared on the road. The crew killed many of them and spent two nights there, and were refreshed and recovered their strength. Their hounds were also fed and revived, for many of them had also become weak with hunger and were left to die by the side of the road. And after this, the men gave much thanks to God, and I became highly esteemed in their eyes. There was food in great abundance from that day forward. They even found wild honey and offered me a taste of it. But then I heard one of them say, "May this be a sacrifice to our gods." Thanks be to the true God, I tasted none of it.

20. Now on that same night, when I was sleeping, Satan attacked me and tempted me violently, in such a powerful way that the memory will remain with me for as long as I inhabit this body. The unholy one fell upon me like a huge rock, and I lost the power of my limbs. But from where did the thought come to my mind to invoke Helias? I know not. But I saw the sun rise in the sky, and I kept shouting "Helias! Helias!" with all my might, and suddenly the splendor of that sun fell on me and freed me of all misery. And I believe that I was sustained by Christ my Lord, and that His Spirit was even then crying out in my behalf. And I hope it will be so on the day of my tribulation, as is written in the Gospel: "On that day," the Lord declares, "it is not you that speaks, but the Spirit of your Father that speaks in you."

21. Yet again, many years later, I was taken captive. So on that first night I stayed with them. I heard a divine message saying to me: "You will be with them for two months more." And it happened that on the sixtieth night after that vision, the Lord delivered me from their hands.

22. On our journey He provided food for us and fire and dry weather every day for ten days until we reached a place where people lived. As I have already told, we traveled through deserted country for twenty-eight days. And on the night we reached our destination it was true that we had no food left.

23. And again after a few years I returned to Britain to be with my kinfolk, who received me as their long-lost son and pleaded with me that now at last, having suffered such difficulties, I should promise them not to go away again.

And there one night I saw a vision of a man, whose name was Victoricus, coming it seemed from Ireland, with countless letters. He gave me one of them, and I read the first words of the letter, which were: "The Voice of the Irish." And as I read aloud the beginning of the letter I imagined that at the same moment I heard their voices— they were those very people who lived hard by the Wood of Foclut, which lies near the Western Sea [where the sun sets]—and thus did they cry out as one: "We ask you, holy boy, come back and walk among us once more."

I was quite brokenhearted and could read no more, and so I woke up. Thanks be to God, after many years the Lord granted to them their desire according to their prayer.

24. And on another night—whether within me or beside me, I know not, only God knows—they [the Irish] called out to me most unmistakably with words that I heard but could not quite understand, except that at the end of the prayer He spoke thus: "He who has laid down His own life for you, it is He who speaks to you." And so I awoke full of joy!

25. Once again [on another night] I saw Him praying within me, and it was as if He were in my body. And I heard Him over me, that is, over my inner self, and He was praying mightily and groaning. All the while I was astonished and amazed, wondering who it could be who was praying within me. But at the end of the prayer, He spoke to me, saying that He was the Spirit. At that I awoke, and I remembered what the apostle had said: "The Spirit helps the weaknesses of our prayers. For we know not what we should pray for or how. But the Spirit Himself intercedes for us with indescribable groanings that cannot be expressed in words." And it is also written: "The Lord Himself is our advocate and asks on our behalf."

26. And when I was attacked by certain of my elders, who came forward and brought up my sins against [as a challenge to] my hard-won episcopate, I was truly on that day so cast down that I might have fallen, now and for all eternity. But the Lord spared His disciple, who has chosen exile for His name's sake, and He came strongly to my aid during this time of humiliation. And since I did not fall badly into disgrace and reproach, and no harm came to me, I pray to God that it will not be reckoned against them [who brought these charges] as a sin.

27. After the lapse of thirty years they [these Churchmen] found a charge against me, raising the words of a confession that I had made just before I was ordained a deacon. When in a state of worry and sadness, I had privately confided to my dearest friend a sin I had committed one day in my youth—in fact, in a single hour of weakness. I cannot say for certain—though God surely knows—if I had yet reached the age of fifteen, and I was still, as I had been since my childhood, not a believer in the living God. But I remained in a state of death and unbelief until I was severely punished by the daily humiliations of hunger and nakedness.

28. Yet, while it was not of my own choice that I traveled to Ireland at the time when I was nearly a lost soul, it was well for me, because I was reformed [corrected] by the Lord, and He made me fit to be today what was once so unlikely and far removed from me: that I, who scarcely thought of my own salvation, should work for and tend to the salvation of others.

29. Thus, on that day when I was rejected by those people I mentioned above, that night I experienced a dream-vision: it was the documents of my dishonor [appearing] before me. And I could hear the voice of God saying to me, "We have seen with unhappiness the face of the chosen one [the bishop of the Irish] stripped of his good name." The voice did not say, "I was displeased to see," but "We were displeased to see"—as though He had joined Himself with me. For it is just as He has said: "He who touches you, it is as if he has touched the apple of My eye."

30. Therefore, I give thanks to Him, who gave me strength in all things, not hindering me from the journey on which I had resolved, or from the difficult task that I had learned from Christ my Lord. Rather, I felt even more His limitless power [and virtue] within me; and my faith was approved before God and men.

31. I say boldly that my conscience does not bother me, neither now nor will it in the future, for I have God as my witness that I have not lied in all I have said to you.

32. Instead I grieve for my closest friend, for how can we [possibly] deserve to hear such evidence given [against me]? To him I had opened up my soul! For I heard from the brethren that before my case was tried—for I myself was not present, nor was I even in Britain for the matter, and it was not at my instigation—it was to be he who would argue on my behalf in my absence. It was even he whose lips had uttered to me, "Look, you should be [are worthy to be] raised to the rank of bishop," though I myself had thought I was not worthy. But how, then, did it occur to him so soon afterwards to shame me in public, in the presence of everyone, good and bad, to heap upon me disgrace for an offense that he had willingly and gladly forgiven—just as had the Lord, who is greater than all men?

33. I have written enough. However, I must not hide God's gift, which he generously gave me in the country of my captivity. Because then I sincerely sought Him and there I found Him. He protected me from evil because, I fervently believe, His Spirit lives within me and works within me even to this day. Yes, I speak this truth boldly, yet God knows if the voice had been that of a man, I might have remained silent for the love of Christ.

34. This is why, never wearied, I tirelessly give thanks to my God, who kept me faithful on the day I was so sorely tried, so that today I can confidently offer Him my soul as a living sacrifice—to Jesus Christ my Lord, who preserved [defended] me from all of my tribulations.

Thus I can say to Him, "Who am I, O Lord, and what have You called me to do, You who assisted me with Your divine power that now I always praise and magnify Your name among the Gentiles wherever I may be, and not only in good days but also in times of danger?" So whatever happens to me, good or evil, I must accept readily and always give thanks to God, who has taught me to believe in Him always without hesitation. He must have heard my prayer so that I, however unworthy I was, should be granted the ability to undertake this holy and wonderful challenge in these last days; in this way I imitate those who, as the Lord foretold long ago, would preach His Gospel as a message to all nations and tribes before the end of the world. So we have seen it happen, and so the prediction has been fulfilled. We ourselves are witnesses that the Gospel has been carried unto those places beyond which no one lives.

35. But now it would be tedious and tiring to relate a detailed accounting of all my works or even parts of them. Let me instead tell you briefly how the most merciful and caring God often freed me from slavery and from twelve dangers that threatened my life—not to mention numerous traps and plots, which I cannot describe in words. I do not wish to bore my readers. Yet God is the authority, who knows all things even before they occur, and He used to advise me in advance, poor ignorant orphan that I am, of many such events by a divine message.

36. How did I come by this wisdom and understanding, which was never within me, who knew not the number of my days nor even knew what God was? When was the gift given to me, so great, so beneficial—to know God and to love Him, although at the price of giving up my native country and my parents?

37. And many gifts were offered to me in sorrow and with tears, and I offended the givers, sometimes against the wishes of my superiors; but, guided by God, in no way did I agree with them nor yield to them. It was not by my own powers, but God's, who prevails within me and makes me resist them all. When I came to the Gentiles of Ireland to preach the Gospel, and to suffer insults from the heathens, hearing the criticisms of my going abroad, and many persecutions, even imprisonment, and to give away my free birthright for the benefit of others—He was with me always. And, should I be deemed worthy, I am prepared to sacrifice my life without hesitation and joyfully for His name, and it is there [in Ireland] that I wish to spend it until I die, if the Lord will allow me to do so.

38. I am very deeply in God's debt, He who gave me such grace that so many people were reborn in God through me and afterward confirmed in the Church, and that priests were ordained for them everywhere, for a people just awakening to faith. They are the Lord's chosen, from the outermost parts of the earth, as He had previously promised through His prophets: "The Gentiles shall come to You from the far ends of the earth, and they shall say, 'How false are the idols that our fathers made for themselves, and there is no use in them.' " And again: "I have set You as a light among the heathen nations, so that You may be the way to salvation even as far as the utmost part of the earth."

39. And there I wish to wait for His promise who surely never disappoints; as He promises in the Gospel: "They will come from the east and the west and they shall sit down with Abraham and Isaac and Jacob"—thus we believe that the faithful will come from the entire world.

40. For that reason we ought to fish well and with diligent care, as the Lord commands and teaches, saying: "Follow Me, and I will make you fishers of men." Again He says through the prophets: "Behold, I send many fishers and hunters, says God," and so on.

This is why it was most necessary to spread our nets widely so that a great throng and multitude might be captured for God, and that there be clergy everywhere to baptize and teach a people who need and want so badly, as the Lord admonishes in the Gospel, saying: "Go now and teach all nations, baptizing them in the name of the Father and of the Son and of the Holy Spirit, teaching them to observe all the things I have taught you; and see, I am with you all days, even until the end of the world." And again He says: "Go out therefore to the whole world and preach the Gospel to every creature. He who believes and is baptized shall be saved, but he who does not believe shall be condemned." And again: "This Gospel of the kingdom shall be preached in the entire world for a testimony to all races of people, and then shall the end come." And so, too, the Lord announces through the prophet, and says: "And it shall come to pass, in the last days, says the Lord, I will pour out my Spirit upon all flesh, and your sons and your daughters shall prophesy, and your young men shall see visions, and your old ones shall dream dreams. And upon my manservants and maidservants I will pour out my Spirit, and they, too, shall prophesy."

Finally, in Hosea He says: "I will call those who were not My people, My people; and those who have not received My mercy, they shall receive My mercy. And where before in the place where it was said, 'You are not my people,' there they shall be called children of the living God."

41. This, then, is how the people of Ireland, who had never had any knowledge of God, but until now had cults and worshiped idols and abominations, have lately been turned into a people of the Lord and are called the children of God. Now the sons of the Irish and the daughters of their kings have openly become monks and virgins of Christ.

42. And there was a special, blessed woman of Irish origin—noble in rank, mature and beautiful—whom I had baptized. She came to us a few days later and told us in private that she had received a message from an angel of God who inspired her to become a virgin of Christ and to draw nearer to Him. Thanks be to God for just six days afterward, she embraced eagerly and sincerely those vows that all the virgins of God follow. They do not have their fathers' consent; rather, they often endure all manner of persecution and false accusations from their own parents. Nevertheless their number increases ever more until we cannot know how many of our race have been thus reborn, as well as the number of widows and women who live a life of chastity.

But the women who are held in slavery—they are the ones who suffer most. They must endure constant threats and terror every day. But the Lord has bestowed His grace on many of these, His handmaids, for although they are forbidden [by their elders], they courageously follow the example of their sisters.

43. So that, even if I wished to leave them and journey to Britain—and I was, with all my heart, ready and anxious to return to my homeland and my parents, and even more, to continue on to Gaul and visit the brethren and be in the presence of the saints of my Lord (how I desired it!)—I am bound by the Spirit, who has testified to me that I should be judged guilty if I were to do this. And I am fearful of destroying the work that I have begun [were I to leave]—and it is not just me, for the Lord Christ commanded me to come and live among them for the rest of my life. I pray it is the Lord's will to protect me from every evil, so that I may not sin in His sight.

44. Now I hope that I have acted as I should have, according to my sacred duty as I see it; but I do not trust myself as long as I am in this mortal body and subject to death—for the flesh is so powerful that it daily tries to turn me from my faith and from the pure teachings of our true religion, which I cling to even if it means the end of my earthly life, for the sake of my Lord Jesus Christ. But the flesh, our enemy, is always dragging us closer to death, that is, toward that which is enticing but forbidden; and I know surely that I have not always led a perfect life as other Christian believers have—I confess this to my Lord and I am not ashamed before Him. He knows that I do not lie. Ever since I first came to know Him in my youth, the fear and love of God have grown within me, so that from that day to this, by the grace of God, I have kept the faith.

45. Let anyone who wishes to laugh and mock me do so, for I will not be silent, nor will I refrain from revealing the signs and wonders that the Lord has shown to me many years before they came to pass, for He knows all that is to occur since before the very beginning of time.

46. Therefore I should give unceasing thanks to God, for He has so often been forgiving of my carelessness and stupidity. More than once—many times—He was not angry with me, though I was slow to accept His choice of me as His servant, even though His will was clearly revealed to me and it was what the Spirit prompted. Indeed the Lord showed mercy to me thousands upon thousands of times, because He saw that I was ready. But I was uncertain how I was to carry out this mission, and many [of my fellows] opposed my mission and were against me. They would talk behind my back and ask each other: "Why does this man dare to thrust himself into danger among the infidels who do not know God?"

It was not out of hatred that they said this—but because they thought it did not make sense and because they thought me uneducated and unworthy, which I myself admit is true. At the time I was not aware of the special grace that was [working] within me. Now I have that wisdom, but I did not have it before.

47. Now then, I have explained simply to my brothers and my fellow servants who have trusted me because of the message I have preached—and continue to preach—in order to strengthen and confirm your faith. Would that my words might encourage you to imitate the higher ideals and to act for the better. This will be my legacy, for "The wise son is the pride of his father."

48. You know, and God knows, too, that I have lived among you since my youth in true faith and with a sincere heart. I have kept faith, and will always keep faith, even with the heathen tribes among whom I live. God knows I have neither cheated nor been false to any of them, nor even thought of doing so, for fear that I would cause them to attack God and His Church, and to persecute all of us, and lest the name of the Lord be blasphemed because of me. For it is written: "Woe to the man through whom the name of the Lord is blasphemed."

49. But though I was untaught in many skills, yet I have done all that I could to protect myself in my dealings with the Christian brethren, with the virgins of Christ, and with the devout women who freely presented me with trinkets or tossed their valuable ornaments onto the altar [for me]. I returned all these gifts to them again, though they were offended because they did not understand my reasons. I acted as I did because of my hope for immortality. By being cautious in all my affairs, unbelievers could not criticize me or tarnish the Church, and I would not, even in the smallest detail, give anyone pretext to discredit or defame my ministry.

50. Is it possible, then, that in the baptizing of so many thousands of people, I received or wished to receive even half a coin [*scriptula*, or scruple] from anyone? Just tell me and I shall repay it to the giver! Or when the Lord, through my very mediocre talents, ordained clergy far and wide, and I conferred His ministry to all without charge—if I asked any of them for so much as the price of a shoe, speak out and I will return it.

51. Instead, it was I who spent on your behalf, so that they would receive me. I traveled among you and went everywhere, often at great personal peril, even to the remotest parts of the land beyond which there is nothing and nobody, where no one had ever come to baptize, to ordain priests, or to confirm the faithful. By the Lord's grace, I have done all this, conscientiously and gladly, for your salvation.

52. At times I gave presents to chiefs, apart from the

sums [wages] I gave their sons to accompany me. Even so, once they arrested me and my companions and were eager to kill me. But my time had not yet come, and they were satisfied to steal all our belongings and bind me in chains. After fourteen days, the Lord delivered me from their power, and our possessions were returned to us, with the help of God and the help of powerful friends whom we had known from before.

53. But you already know how much I have paid to the administrators and judges of all the districts I visited regularly [for their protection]. I estimate that I must have paid no less than the price of fifteen men [slaves] so that you may safely continue to enjoy my ministry and I may continue to enjoy you in God. I have no regrets, nor is it enough, for I continue to spend and will pay even more. The Lord has the power to grant me the will that I may eventually spend my very soul for the sake of your souls.

54. With all my soul I call upon my God to witness that I do not lie. Neither, I hope, am I writing to you in order to flatter or to gain something I do not deserve, nor because I look for praise from any of you. Sufficient is the honor that is not yet seen but is held in the heart. But He who promised is faithful; He never lies.

55. But I see I am already exalted in this time and place beyond measure by the Lord. And I was not worthy nor such a man that He should award me this gift. I know perfectly well that poverty and misfortune suit me better than wealth and pleasures. For Christ the Lord, too, was poor for our sakes; and I, unhappy failure that I am, have no riches even if I wished it so. I do not judge myself, because daily I expect to be murdered, betrayed, or captured, or whatever disaster may await me; but I fear none of these things, because of the promises of heaven. I have thrown myself into the hands of God Almighty, who reigns everywhere. As the prophet says: "Cast your care upon God, and He shall answer your need."

56. Look, now I commend my soul to my faithful God, for whom I am an ambassador, despite my ignoble obscurity; He accepts no person of his own accord, but He *chose* me for this office—to be one of His ministers, although the lowest.

57. How shall I repay the Lord for all He has bestowed upon me? But what shall I say, what shall I promise to God, since I have no power except what He gives to me? But only let Him look into my deepmost heart: He will see that I am willing and ready for Him to grant me a drink from His chalice, as He has permitted others who also love Him.

58. Therefore, may God never allow me to lose His people whom He has won at the farthest corners of the earth. I pray that God will grant his humble son perseverance and will allow me to give faithful testimony of Him until the time of my own passing, all for the sake of my God.

59. And if I ever achieved any good for the sake of the Lord whom I love, I beseech that I may be allowed to shed my blood with those [other] exiles and prisoners for His name, even if it means I am denied burial and that my miserable body will be torn limb from limb by dogs or wild beasts, or devoured by birds of the air. For I confidently believe that if this were to happen to me, I have gained my soul for the price of my body, for on that day we shall surely arise in the brilliance of the sun, that is, in the glory of Christ Jesus our Redeemer, as children of the living God and coheirs with Christ, to be formed in His image; since through Him, with Him, and in Him we shall reign.

60. For that sun, which we see rising every day, rises at His command; but it will never rule over the universe, nor will its splendor last forever. And all those who worship it will end in misery and receive terrible punishment. But not we, who believe in and worship the true sun, Christ; He shall never die, and neither will anyone who does His will—instead, he shall live forever, just as Christ lives forever, who reigns with God the Father Almighty and with the Holy Spirit since before the beginning of time and forever after. Amen.

61. Behold, again and again, I wrote down what I wish to declare in my confession. I testify truthfully and with great joy in my heart before God and His holy angels that I have never had any motive for returning to the land from which I had long ago barely escaped other than the [preaching of the] Gospel and [teaching of] its promises.

62. But I pray that all those who believe in and fear God, whoever discovers this document and reads these words, composed in Ireland by an unlearned sinner named Patrick—let no one ever say that what little I have accomplished was the work of this ignorant man alone. No, rather, know this and believe this: that it was a gift from God, that it occurred only for God's good reasons. And that is my confession before I die.

Appendix B
The Letter to the
Soldiers of Coroticus

1. I, Patrick, a sinner and poorly learned, as is well known, speak to you as the true and anointed bishop in Ireland. I believe with certainty that all that I am I have received from God; and so I live among barbarians and foreigners, a stranger and an exile for the love of the Father—and He is my witness that this is so. I would never, of my own will, speak so harshly and sternly as I feel I must, but I am compelled to by the zeal of God and the truth of Christ, and for the love for my friends [neighbors] and children [sons], for whom I have given up my homeland and my family, and even risked my very life unto the point of death. Though I am despised by some, I have dedicated my life— if I am worthy—to my God to teach these heathen tribes.

2. I have written these words myself and sent them to be given, delivered, and handed to the soldiers of Coroticus. I do not call them my own people nor fellow citizens of the holy Romans, but because of their evil deeds [I call them] the cohorts of demons. As enemies of God, they are dead even while they are alive, allies of the Scots [i.e., Irish] and the outlaw Picts, who are apostates. I denounce them as bloodthirsty men who seek to gorge themselves on the blood of innocent Christians, whom I have "given birth to" [begotten] in countless numbers for God and confirmed in Christ.

3. On the day after the newly baptized, still wearing white garments and freshly anointed, were butchered—the chrism [oil] was still fragrant and shone on their foreheads as they were cruelly slaughtered by the swords of the marauders I have just mentioned—I sent a letter with a holy priest whom I had instructed from his childhood, accompanied by other priests, imploring them to return some of the booty and baptized captives to us. They laughed in the faces of my emissaries.

4. Therefore, I do not know for whom I should more rightly grieve. Should I weep for those who were killed or captured, or for those whom the devil has enslaved? For they will be bound along with him [Satan] to the eternal pains of hell, since one who commits a mortal sin is himself a slave and is called the son of Satan.

5. So let every God-fearing person know that those who murder their own families, who kill their brothers like ravening wolves, who devour the people of the Lord as they would eat bread—they are forever estranged from me and from my God, whose missionary I am. As is said, "The wicked have destroyed Your law, O Lord," the law that He has of late—and at the end of time—graciously sown so successfully in Ireland to become firmly established there with God's grace.

6. I make no false accusation. [I do not exceed my au-

thority.] I am the one He has called and preordained to preach the Gospel despite so many serious persecutions and even to the very ends of the earth, and though the enemy shows his disdain for me through the actions of the tyrant Coroticus, who fears neither God nor the clergy [priests and bishops], whom He has chosen and whom He has granted the highest spiritual power to bind in heaven those whom they bind on earth.

7. Therefore I earnestly beseech those of you who are holy and humble of heart that it is not correct to seek favor from such as their kind, or even to eat or drink with them, nor should alms be accepted from them until they have done the most severe penance, pouring out their tears to God's satisfaction, and until they have freed the baptized servants and handmaidens of Christ on whose behalf He died and was crucified.

8. Scripture tells us, "The Almighty utterly rejects the gifts of the wicked. He that offers as a sacrifice the property taken from the poor is like a man who sacrifices the son in the sight of the father." It is said that, "The wealth that he has accumulated criminally he shall vomit up from his belly. The angel of death will drag him away and he will be tormented by wrathful dragons; the snake's tongue shall kill him and an unending fire will consume him." And thus, "Woe be to those who sate themselves with what is not their own," and "What shall it profit a man to gain the world and suffer the loss of his own soul?"

9. It would be tedious and boring to lay out in detail their crimes and to quote from the texts of the whole Law that proscribe such greed. Suffice it to declare that avarice is a mortal sin. Remember, "You shall not covet your neighbor's goods" and "You shall not kill." We know that a murderer cannot stand with Christ. And he who hates his brother will be called a murderer, and "He who hates his brother lives in death." More offensive is he who stains his hands with the blood of those children of God whom He has recently won over to His ways through my own paltry efforts here at the utmost ends of the earth.

10. Could I have come here, to Ireland, without the guidance of God, or for reasons that were human and secular? Who compelled me on this mission? It is because of the Holy Spirit that I am bound to remain forever separated from my family. Does this forgiveness that I have shown to the very people who once enslaved me and pillaged the male and female servants of my father's household come from within me? In the eyes of the secular world, I am a free man, the son of a Roman decurion. But I have traded my noble birthright, without shame or second thought, for the advantage [benefit] of others. In a word, I am Christ's slave; I serve Him by ministering to foreign tribes for the sake of the indescribable glory of eternal life that is in Christ Jesus our Lord.

11. And if my own people will not know [appreciate] me, it is because "a prophet is without honor in his own country." Indeed, perhaps we are not of the same fold and do not have the one true God. As He says: "He who is not with Me is against Me, and he who does not gather with Me, scatters." It is not enough [not correct] that one destroys and another builds up. I do not seek anything for myself. It was not by my own grace, but God who put within me this sincere care in my heart, that I should be one of His hunters and fishers of souls, whom God had long ago foretold would come in the end of days.

12. I am the target of resentment and jealousy. What shall I do, O Lord? I am openly despised. Look, all around me Your sheep lie torn and spoiled, and by these very soldiers of Coroticus at his evil orders. Far removed from the love of God is anyone who betrays my newly won Christian into the hands of the Scots and Picts. Voracious wolves have eaten the Lord's flock, just when it was increasing in Ireland with tender care. How many sons of Scots kings and daughters of Pictic chiefs have become monks and virgins of Christ—I cannot count their number. So do not be pleased by this calamity; it is unacceptable, unjust, and irredeemable all the way to hell.

13. So who among the holy saints would not shudder to make merry or partake of a feast with men such as these? They have filled their houses with the stolen property of dead Christians; they live only to plunder. These wretched men do not know that it is poison that they offer as food to their children and their friends, just as Eve did not realize that it was certain death she was offering to her husband. But so it is always with those who commit such evil: their earthly work brings only the eternal punishment of death.

14. However, the custom of the Christian Romans of Gaul is different: they send holy and capable men to the Franks and other heathen nations with as many thousands of *solidi* as required to ransom baptized captives. But you [Coroticus] murder them or sell them to a foreign race who do not know of our true God; you might as well hand over the members of Christ to a brothel. What hope could you then have in the grace of God, or could anyone have who agrees with you, or who speaks with you, or who shows you any measure of respect? God Himself will surely judge. For it is written, "Not only those who do evil, but those who consent to it will be condemned."

15. I do not know what more I should say or how I can

speak of those dead children of God who were ruthlessly struck down by the sword. For it is written: "Weep with those who weep." And again: "If one member grieves, let all be sorrowful." Therefore the entire Church weeps and mourns her sons and daughters whom the sword has not yet touched [slain], but who were made into slaves and taken to distant lands where terrible sin abounds, openly, wickedly, and without shame. Freeborn men are sold there and Christians enslaved—and, worst of all, they are sold to the most despicable and apostate Picts.

16. For this reason I cry aloud in sadness and grief: O most beautiful and beloved brothers and sons whom I confirmed in Christ, and whom I cannot number, what shall I do for you now? I am unworthy to help either God or man. The injustice of wicked men has overcome us. It has made us strangers to one another. Perhaps they do not believe that we have received the same baptism, or that we have the same God and the same Father. They look down at us because we are Irish. But the prophet said: "Have you not the one God? Why have you—each and every one of you— forsaken your neighbor?"

17. Consequently, I grieve for you. Indeed, I deeply mourn for you, my dearly beloved ones. Yet, I also rejoice within myself. For I see that I have not labored without result, and my journey [exile] to an alien land was not without purpose. And though this was an unspeakably horrible crime, I thank God that you were baptized believers when you left this world for paradise. I can see you in a vision: you have embarked upon your journey to a place where there is no more night, no sorrow, and no death. Freed from your chains, you will romp like young lambs and the wicked will be like ashes beneath your feet.

18. You will reign with the apostles and the prophets and the martyrs. You will win eternal kingdoms, just as He Himself promised: "They shall come from the east and west, and they shall sit with Abraham, Isaac, and Jacob in the kingdom of heaven." While "outside [heaven] lie the dogs, the evildoers, and the murderers." And "liars and blasphemers shall be damned to the lake of eternal fire." The apostle rightly says: "When the just man shall barely be saved, where will the sinner and the ungodly lawbreaker expect to find himself?"

19. Where, then, will Coroticus and his criminal band, all of them rebels against Christ—where do they see themselves [in the end]? They have given away baptized young women as booty, all for the miserable earthly gain [of money] that will pass away in a moment like a cloud or a wisp of smoke dispersed by the wind. These wicked sinners will evaporate in the presence of the Lord, but the just will certainly feast with Christ. They will sit in judgment of the nations and rule over unjust kings for ever and ever. Amen.

20. I witness before God and His angels that, though I lack learning, all shall be as I have predicted. For these words that I have written in Latin are not mine; they are from God and His apostles and prophets, who have never lied. "Whoever believes will be saved; whoever does not believe will be damned." Thus God has spoken.

21. My first and sincerest request is that the servants of God who shall come into possession of this letter, do not conceal or withdraw it, but be sure that it is read aloud in public, and even when Coroticus himself is there. I pray that God will inspire the hearers to come to their senses and, even at this late stage, that they should repent of the evil they have committed—the murder of the Lord's brothers—and that they should release the baptized women whom they had taken prisoner and sold. In this way they may yet deserve to live in the grace of God, and they may be restored whole, here and for all eternity. Peace be to the Father, to the Son, and to the Holy Spirit. Amen.

APPENDIX C
THE LORICA OF ST. PATRICK

The word *Lorica* is Latin and was used in ancient Ireland to denote a piece of armor, usually a breastplate. This prayer is included here not so much because it is a work by St. Patrick; it certainly was not composed in its present form by Patrick, and any way in which it was inspired by Patrick or his legacy leads through at least two centuries of strictly oral tradition. In fact, there were many Loricas used by Christians in the early medieval period as prayer forms or as hymns. This one has been ascribed to St. Patrick because of its archaic qualities and because it so resolutely upholds the Trinitarian view of God, an important theme in the writings we are certain are from the hand of Patrick.

The protective quality of the Lorica was likely derived from earlier pagan rituals in which people could be rendered invisible to their enemies, and the legend attached to the prayer is that its recitation was used by Patrick to make his entourage traveling through the forests appear to be a herd of wild deer to the soldiers of King Laoghaire, son of Niall. Following this herd was a young fawn: it was Benin (later St. Benignus), the young disciple of St. Patrick who would later succeed him in the see of Armagh. And it was this fawn that, legend has it, bleated out the prayer that became the Lorica; hence the prayer is also called *Feth Fiada*, the "Deer's Cry."

The prayer has been recognized as having a simplicity and an eloquence that set it apart, and its recitation has for centuries been a source of protection—from what? From the intrusion of the world into faith. The prayer's form, like a suit of armor, has had the power to insulate the worshiper from the powers, the mists, that seep into the mind and the soul and bring them into the din of the world. The prayer creates a calm in which the worshiper can commune with one's own soul and find both faith and serenity. I find no difficulty associating the prayer with Patrick. I hear the same voice in it that I hear when I read the *Confession* or the *Letter*.

This translation is one of at least a score that are available in Patrician literature of the past one hundred years.

The Lorica (Breastplate) of St. Patrick (The *Feth Fiada* or "Deer's Cry")

I

I arise today:
> vast in might, invocation of the Trinity;
> belief in a Threeness;
> confession of Oneness;
> meeting in the Creator.

II

I arise today:
> in the might of Christ's Birth and His Baptism;

in the might of His Crucifixion and Burial;
in the might of His Resurrection and Ascension;
in the might of His Descent to the Judgment of
Doom.

III

I arise today:
in the might of the Cherubim;
in obedience of Angels;
in ministration of Archangels;
in hope of resurrection through merit;
in prayers of Patriarchs;
in predictions of Prophets;
in preachings of Apostles;
in faiths of Confessors;
in innocence of holy Virgins;
in deeds of good men.

IV

I arise today:
in the might of Heaven;
Splendor of the Sun;
whiteness of Snow;
irresistibleness of Fire;
the swiftness of Lightning;
the speed of Wind;
Absoluteness of the Deep;
Earth's stability;
Rock's durability.

V

I arise today:
in the might of God   for my piloting;
Power of God   for my stability;
Wisdom of God   for my guidance;
Eye of God   for my foresight;
Ear of God   for my hearing;

Word of God   for my word [speaking];
Hand of God   for my guard;
Path of God   for my prevention;
Shield of God   for my protection;
Host of God   for my salvation;
    against every demon's snare;
    against all vices' lure;
    against concupiscence;
    against ill-wishes far and near.

VI

I invoke all these forces:
    between me and every savage force that may come
      upon me, body and my soul;
    against incantations of false prophets;
    against black laws of paganism;
    against false laws of heresy;
    against idolatry;
    against spells of women and smiths and druids;
    against all knowledge that should not be known.

VII

Christ for my guard today:
    against poison, against burning,
    against drowning, against wounding,
  that there may come to me merit;

VIII

Christ with me, Christ before me,
Christ behind me, Christ in me,
Christ under me, Christ over me,
Christ to the right of me, Christ to the left of me,
Christ in lying down, Christ in sitting, Christ in rising up;

IX

Christ in all, who may think of me!
Christ in the mouth of all who may speak to me!

Christ in the eye, that may look on me!
Christ in the ear, that may hear me!

X

I arise today:
    in vast might, of the Trinity prayed to:
    believing on a Threeness;
    confessing a Oneness:
    meeting in the Creator;
Domini est salus, Domini est salus, Christi est salus;
Salus tua, Domine, sit semper nobiscum.
[Salvation is the Lord's, salvation is the Lord's, salvation
    is Christ's;
May Thy salvation, O Lord, be always with us.]

[TRANSLATION FROM GOGARTY,
I FOLLOW SAINT PATRICK, PP. 251–253]

APPENDIX D
THE HYMN OF SECUNDINUS

The *Confession of St. Patrick* and the *Letter to the Soldiers of Coroticus* are certainly documents from the hand of St. Patrick; the Lorica is almost certainly a prayer composed well after Patrick's time, but has, since antiquity, been associated with the legacy and persona of Patrick as those have imbued the life and soil of Ireland. The *Hymn of Secundinus* is a document that falls in between these verities: it probably was composed close to Patrick's time, and the tradition that it came from the period in between the composition of the *Letter* and the *Confession* is supported by some internal evidence.

Secundinus was certainly a real person; he was one of three bishops (the others being Auxilius and Iserninus) sent to Ireland to assist Patrick in his ministry. Many legends surround Secundinus (including one in which Secundinus and Patrick are one and the same), but we know almost nothing about him with any degree of certainty.

What has survived is this hymn, which was written, it is said, by Secundinus in an effort to capture the presence of his master. Since before the name of Patrick became celebrated in the Church of Ireland, the hymn was used to invoke the spirit and legacy of the man.

Written as an alphabetical acrostic, the first letter of each stanza title (in Latin) is a consecutive letter of the alphabet. In this, it has the same incantation quality of the Lorica—a prayer that invokes memories and spirit of a teacher and saint, more a record of a spiritual legacy than a ledger entry in a census book. In many versions, and in my mind, the description "Teacher of the Irish" is appended to the title. I have always found this apt, because it reminds me that the hymn is the product of a disciple's appreciation of his master.

The Hymn of St. Patrick, Teacher of the Irish by Secundinus

Audite (Listen)

Hear all ye who love God, the holy merits
Of the Bishop Patrick, a man blessed in Christ;
How, on account of his good actions, he is likened unto
    the angels,
And for his perfect life, is counted equal to the
    Apostles.

Beati (O You Blessed)

He keepeth the commandments of the blessed Christ in
    all things,
His works shine brightly before men,
Who follow his holy and admirable example,
Whence also they glorify the Lord his Father which is
    in heaven.

Constans (Perseverance)

Steadfast in the fear of the Lord, and immovable in faith;
On whom, as on Peter, the Church is built;
Who received his Apostleship from God.
The gates of hell shall not prevail against him.

Dominus (The Lord)

The Lord chose him to teach the barbarous nations,
To fish (for men) with the nets of doctrine,
To draw believers from the world unto grace,
That they might follow the Lord to the heavenly seat.

Electa (The Chosen)

He trades with the choice Gospel talents of Christ,
Which he puts out at usury amongst the Hibernian
    nations,
Destined hereafter, along with Christ, to possess the joy
    of the heavenly kingdom,
As a recompense for this labor.

Fidelis (The Faithful)

A faithful messenger and distinguished messenger
    of God,
He shows to the good an apostolic example and
    pattern;
Who preaches to the people of God, as well by deeds as
    by words,
So that by good works he may provoke those to
    imitation, whom he does not convert by his words.

Gloriam (Glory [to God])

He has glory with Christ, and honor in this world,
Being venerated by all as the angel of God;
Whom God sent, even as Paul, to be an Apostle to the
    Gentiles,
To guide men unto the kingdom of God.

Humilis (Humility)

Humble, through fear of God, both in spirit and
    behavior,
Upon whom an account of his good actions rests the
    Spirit of the Lord:
Who beareth in his righteous flesh the marks of Christ,
In whose cross alone he glories and sustains himself.

Impiger (The Deprived)

He diligently feedeth believers with heavenly food
Lest those who are seen with Christ should faint by
    the way:
To whom he distributes the words of the Gospel like
    the loaves
In whose hands they are multiplied like the manna.

Kastam (Purity)

Who, through the love of God, keepeth his flesh pure,
Having prepared it to be a temple for the Holy Spirit,
By whom it is constantly possessed with good motions;
And who offers up his body a living sacrifice, well-
    pleasing to the Lord.

Lumen (The Light)

He is a great and burning evangelical light of the world,
Set upon a candlestick, shining unto the whole world;
A strong city of the king, set upon a hill,
In which is much store of the riches of the Lord.

Maximus (Greatness)

He shall be called the greatest in the kingdom of heaven
Who fulfills, by good works, what he teaches in his
    holy discourses.
He goes before with a good example, and a pattern to
    the faithful;
And in a pure heart has faith towards God.

Nomen (The Name)

He boldly preaches the name of the Lord to the
      Gentiles,
To whom he gives the eternal grace of the laver of
      salvation;
For whose offenses he daily prays to God:
For whom also he offers up sacrifices worthy of God.

Omnem (Christ is All)

He despises all the glory of the world, in comparison
      with the Divine law,
Counting all things as but chaff, compared with Christ's
      table;
Nor is he disturbed by the violence of the thunder of
      this world;
But rejoices in tribulation when he suffers for Christ.

Pastor (The Shepherd)

A good and faithful shepherd of the Gospel-flock,
Chosen by God, to watch the people of God,
And to feed, with Divine doctrines, the nation;
For which, after the example of Christ, he is giving
      his life.

Quem (Whom)

Whom the Savior advanced for his merits, to be a
      Bishop,
That he might exhort the clergy in the heavenly
      warfare;
To whom he distributes the bread from heaven, along
      with garments,
Which is fulfilled in his divine and holy discourses.

Regis (The King)

A messenger of the king, inviting believers to the
      marriage,

Who is arrayed in the wedding garment;
Who draws the heavenly wine in heavenly vessels,
Pledging the people of God in the spiritual cup.

Sacrum (Blessed [or Sacred] Things)

He finds in the sacred volume a sacred treasure,
Which he purchases with his holy and perfect merits.
He discerns also the Godhead of the Savior in the
    flesh.
He is named Israel, beholding God in his spirit.

Testis (Witness)

A faithful witness of God in the Catholic doctrine,
Whose words are seasoned with the Divine oracles,
So that they are not corrupted, like human flesh, and
    eaten of worms;
But are salted with a heavenly savor for the sacrifice.

Verus (The Gospel or Truth)

A true and excellent cultivator of the Gospel field,
Whose seeds are seen to be the Gospels of Christ,
Which he sows from his divine mouth in the ears of
    the wise,
And tills their hearts and minds with the Holy Spirit.

Xristus (The Christ)

Christ chose him to be his vicar on the earth,
Who liberates captives from a two-fold bondage;
And of the many whom he has redeemed from the
    bondage of men,
Releases numberless persons from the dominion of the
    devil.

Ymnos (Hymn)

He sings Hymns, with the Apocalypse, and the Psalms
    of God,

On which also he discourses, for the edification of the
    people of God;
Which Scripture he believes in the Trinity of the
    sacred Name,
And teaches the One substance in Three Persons.

Zona (The Lord's Territory)

Girt with the girdle of the Lord, by day and night,
He prays without ceasing to the Lord God,
Receiving the reward of which great labor,
He shall reign with the Holy Apostles over Israel.

[TRANSLATION FROM OLDEN,
THE EPISTLES AND HYMN OF ST. PATRICK]

Bibliographical Sources

The proliferation of books on just about everything in the latter part of the twentieth century—along with certain happy and unhappy circumstances of the publishing industry during that period—has had, as one of its consequences, the disappearance of books from the shelves that are enjoyable and enlightening reading experiences. The reprint houses cannot keep up with the number of fine titles that go out of print, and libraries are continually under pressure to modernize and streamline their holdings, so that once a book goes out of print, it has a difficult time reappearing regardless of its merit. These facts apply no less to the subject of St. Patrick, so that it may be difficult to obtain copies of many of the titles listed in this (or any other) bibliography through the routine avenues.

For a time it seemed the only recourse was to resign oneself to rummaging through used and antiquarian bookshops, and as pleasurable as that may be for some, it is not a very efficient way of finding just the title one is seeking. Fortunately, modern technology, which certainly deserves to share some of the blame for the current state of affairs, has also provided a recourse and a possible solution: the Internet. A number of services and Web sites exist that will help the modern reader locate and obtain books out of print and undeservedly forgotten—or, in many instances, simply unavailable.

Tom Cahill's masterly volume on early medieval Ireland is as good and entertaining a way to begin, to be complemented by several equally entertaining and inspiring biographical works: a fine piece of writing by Paul Gallico and an engrossing book by E. A. Thompson, which also has (as do many other works here listed) a fine bibliography. There are several ways of obtaining more of St. Patrick's writings and the literature of the age—works stretching from Bieler and MacNeill to Harney, Skinner, and Howlett (the Harney work being a particular favorite)—but one owes it to oneself to be sure to see Liam de Paor's annotated collection at some point in one's reading.

Learning about St. Patrick means looking into the history of his age, and here one can profit from a reading of Bury's pathbreaking biography as well as from the works of Scherman, Williams, and Hughes. The literature regarding the Celtic church and the druidic religion of late ancient Ireland is growing by the minute. Frank Delaney's book and the books listed therein are certainly worthwhile, as are the several books on the subject authored by Miranda Green.

The scholarly study of St. Patrick also begins with Bury (happily being rediscovered as an outstanding scholar in a number of areas) and is developed with academic precision by Hanson (though one wonders if it would have hurt anyone for the many Latin passages to have appeared in translation). The legendary view of St. Patrick is developed in very early works—the rare works by Cusack and Todd, and of course the oft-printed MacManus—and finds a pleasant home in many more modern sophisticated books. A work that doesn't fit easily into any category (as, indeed, neither did the author) is Gogarty's account of his spiritual journey of discovery. A similar tour through the land and its spirit is De Breffny's work. These last two works are the kind of book one reads over and over for the sheer pleasure of it.

Bieler, Ludwig, Ph.D. *The Life and Legend of St. Patrick: Problems of Modern Scholarship.* Dublin: Clonmore and Reynolds, Ltd., 1949.

———. *The Works of St. Patrick.* Westminster, Maryland: The Newman Press, 1953.

Bury, J.B. *The Life of St. Patrick and His Place in History.* London and New York: Macmillan and Co., 1905.

Cahill, Thomas. *How the Irish Saved Civilization.* New York: Doubleday, 1995.

Cusack, M.F. *The Life of St. Patrick, Apostle of Ireland.* Kenmare, County Kerry: National Publication Office, 1869.

De Breffny, Brian. *In the Steps of St. Patrick.* London and New York: Thames and Hudson, 1982.

De Blácam, Hugh. *Gentle Ireland: An Account of a Christian Culture in History and Modern Life.* Milwaukee: The Bruce Publishing Co., 1935.

———. *Saint Patrick: Apostle of Ireland.* Milwaukee: The Bruce Publishing Co., 1941.

Delaney, Frank. *The Celts.* Boston: Little, Brown, 1986.

de Paor, Liam. *Saint Patrick's World: The Christian Culture of Ireland's Apostolic Age.* Dublin: Four Courts Press, 1993.

Ellis, Peter Berresford. *The Druids.* Grand Rapids, Michigan: William B. Eerdsmans, 1994.

Gallico, Paul. *The Steadfast Man: A Biography of St. Patrick.* Garden City, New York: Doubleday and Co., 1958.

Gogarty, Oliver St. John. *I Follow Saint Patrick.* New York: Reynal and Hitchcock, 1938.

Good News Bible: Today's English Version. New York: American Bible Society, 1992.

Green, Miranda J. *The World of the Druids.* London: Thames and Hudson, 1997.

Gubbins, Rev. George Gough. "What Doctrines and Practices Did St. Patrick Teach?" Dublin: J. Charles & Son, 1889.

Hanson, R.P.C. *Saint Patrick: His Origins and Career.* New York and Oxford: Oxford University Press, 1968.

———. *The Life and Writings of the Historical Saint Patrick.* New York: The Seabury Press, 1983.

Harney, Martin P., S.J. *The Legacy of Saint Patrick.* Boston: St. Paul Editions, 1972.

Hopkin, Alannah. *The Living Legend of St. Patrick.* New York: St. Martin's Press, 1989.

Howlett, D.R. *The Confession of Saint Patrick.* Liguori, Missouri: Triumph Books, 1994.

Hughes, Kathleen. *Early Christian Ireland: Introduction to the Sources.* Ithaca, New York: Cornell University Press, 1972.

John Paul II. *In the Footsteps of St. Patrick.* Boston: St. Paul Editions, 1979.

Keyes, Frances Parkinson. *Tongues of Fire.* New York: Coward-McCann, 1966.

Leslie, Shane. *St. Patrick's Purgatory: A Record from History and Literature.* London: Burns, Oates & Washbourne Ltd., 1932.

MacManus, Seumas. *The Story of the Irish Race.* New York: Devin-Adair, 1944.

MacNeill, Eoin. *Saint Patrick.* Dublin: Clonmore and Reynolds, Ltd., 1964.

Ó Cróinín, Dáibhí. *Early Medieval Ireland: 400–1200.* London: Longman, 1995.

O'Curry, Eugene. The Manuscript Materials of Ancient Irish History: Delivered at the Catholic Univ. of Ireland, during the Sessions of 1855 and 1856. London: James Duffy, 1861.

Ó hÓgáin, Dáithi. *Myth, Legend and Romance: An Encyclopedia of the Irish Folk Tradition.* London: Ryan, 1990.

Olden, Rev. Thomas, ed. *The Epistles and Hymn of Saint Patrick.* Dublin: Hodges, Foster & Co., 1876.

Patricius, Magonus Sucatus (St. Patrick). *Confession.*

———. *Letter to the Soldiers of Coroticus.*

Secundinus. *The Hymn of St. Patrick: Teacher of the Irish.*

Scherman, Katharine. *The Flowering of Ireland: Saints, Scholars, and Kings.* Boston: Little, Brown and Co., 1981.

Skinner, John. *The Confession of Saint Patrick.* New York: Doubleday, 1998.

Stokes, George Thomas. *Ireland and the Celtic Church: A History of Ireland from St. Patrick to the English Conquest in 1172.* London: Hodder and Stoughton, 1888.

Thompson, E.A. *Who Was Saint Patrick?* New York: St. Martin's Press, 1985.

Todd, J.H. *St. Patrick, Apostle of Ireland: A Memoir of His Life and Mission.* Dublin: Hodges, Smith & Co., 1864.

Whiteside, Lesley. *The Spirituality of St. Patrick.* Dublin: The Columba Press, 1997.

Williams, Derek. *The Reach of Rome: A History of the Roman Imperial Frontier, 1st–5th Centuries A.D.* New York: St. Martin's Press, 1997.

About the Author

GREG TOBIN is the author of several works of fiction, which include *Jericho*, *Big Horn*, and *Prairie*, all western novels published by Ballantine Books. *The Wisdom of St. Patrick* is his first nonfiction book. He is currently editing an anthology of American Catholic writers and writing a novel. Mr. Tobin is vice president and editor in chief of Book-of-the-Month Club and has been a book-publishing professional for nearly twenty years. He lives in South Orange, New Jersey, with his family, and is a member of Our Lady of Sorrows Parish.